C0-AKJ-467

FENWAY VOICES

FENWAY VOICES

BY JACK LAUTIER

Camden, Maine

To the memory of
Smoky Joe Wood,
a true Hall of Famer!

© 1990 by Jack Lautier.
All rights reserved.
No part of this book may be reproduced or transmitted in any form or by any means, electronic or mechanical, including photocopying, recording, or by any information storage and retrieval system, without the written permission of the publisher, except by a reviewer quoting brief passages in a magazine, newspaper, or broadcast. Address inquiries to Yankee Books, P.O. Box 1248, Camden, Maine 04843.

Cover design by James Pavlovich
Back cover photograph by Steve Lipofsky
Photo page 1 courtesy of the Wood Collection
Photos pages 29, 49, 61, 75, 87, 123, 129, 149, 153 courtesy of *The Sporting News*
Photos pages 71, 101,107, 177, 183 courtesy of the Boston Red Sox
Front cover photo of Ted Williams, courtesy of the Beittmann Archives
Front cover photo of Smoky Joe, courtesy of the Bob Wood Collection
Front cover photo of Roger Clemens, courtesy of the *Globe* file photo

Library of Congress Cataloging-in-Publication Data

Lautier, Jack, 1952–
    Fenway voices : from "Smoky" Joe to "Rocket" Roger / by Jack Lautier.
      p.   cm.
    ISBN 0-89909-324-8
    1. Boston Red Sox (Baseball team)–History.   I. Title.
    GV875.B62L35 1990
    796.357'64'0974461 – dc20   90-36201
                                            CIP

10 9 8 7 6 5 4 3 2

Table of Contents

Foreword

As the former radio voice of the Boston Red Sox, I had the distinct privilege of informing baseball fans of New England and beyond the pitch-by-pitch happenings from Fenway Park.

When I returned to my native port of Quincy, Massachusetts, after a stint doing play-by-play for the Cleveland Indians, I attempted to be a companion for Red Sox fans. As a youngster, my neighborhood was filled with Red Sox loyalists. Truthfully, I have always found something special about Fenway Park, be it sitting in the bleachers several years ago or from pressbox level. It is funny but I feel a rebirth of sorts every time I enter the ballpark.

I guess there is a mechanism in all of us which triggers the mind, soul and memory when a colleague, a neighbor or a relative mentions the Red Sox. It is as if one travels back to a time like it was...the April evening when Roger Clemens struck out 20 Seattle batters to set a major league record...the hot June night in Detroit when Fred Lynn hit three home runs at Tiger Stadium...the final at-bat for Ted Williams at Fenway Park...the roar of the crowd on each hit by Carl Yastrzemski during the pennant chase of the "Impossible Dream" season.

As I write this, each reference has file cards of information flipping in my mind. I suppose the association between people and events is what links the Red Sox to all of us. It is true that names, faces and numbers change each season, but baseball remains the eternal constant, a daily historical entry. From my perch at Fenway Park, my goal was to bring my radio audience closer to the play, as if he or she is sharing the seat next to me. When I said "Dwight Evans belts one, high into the screen in left," I'm hopeful that my listeners painted a mental picture from my words and could see the baseball leaving Dewey's bat, taking flight and landing into the netting atop the Green Monster.

In *Fenway Voices*, the reader will feel the same way. You are assigned a locker in the Boston clubhouse or a seat in the dugout next to the manager. You will hear first-hand what those who were there felt, involved in the action, on the field or on the bench.

Taking his veteran journalistic expertise to a new dimension, Jack Lautier has weaved an oral account of the Boston Red Sox through the reflections of players. What follows is more than a collection of personalities whom Red Sox and baseball fans have treasured over the decades. The anecdotes will take the reader to the Red Sox batting cage. . . to the seventh game of the October Classic. . . to home plate for the playoff games of 1948 and 1978. . . to the mound with a rookie pitcher making his World Series debut. . . along with a batting champion as he makes peace with a rival fan. . . the struggle an athlete must come to grips with once the cheering stops. At times, you will swear Ted Williams is offering you a tip about hitting as he did to several teammates during his career with the Red Sox. The same holds true for the 35 other players contained in this work. What Smoky Joe Wood accomplished as a hard-throwing pitcher for the Red Sox at the turn of the century comes full circle as Roger Clemens ushers the franchise into the 1990s.

It was a pleasure for me to write the opening for *Fenway Voices*. I found the task quite similar to my pre-game baseball radio show. As you recall, before each game, a player and myself would exchange thoughts and ideas as the Boston Red Sox made last minute preparations to engage battle against a long-time American League rival. Well, fans, it looks like this pitcher has completed his warmup tosses. History is waiting, be it another night for Wade Boggs in his pursuit for 200 hits or the Red Sox moving a game closer to another pennant.

Ken Coleman

Cohasset, Massachusetts

Introduction

Fenway Park, the antique shrine of New England, has remained center stage for baseball for generations who come watch the Boston Red Sox. Though plenty has been written about the Red Sox, I can only hope that this book will offer readers another way to be entertained by the players of the Olde Towne Team.

One way to get a seat closer to the action is to talk with those involved. What follows is a collection of interviews of past and present players, the supergreats and greats, who created the thrills and essentially compiled the history of the Red Sox franchise.

Since 1982, I have written several newspaper columns from many of the interviews contained in this volume. After further examination of the conversations with the players, the prospect of doing an oral history of players' reflections came into promise when a book proposal sent by David Black, my agent, met a positive word from editor Linda Spencer at Yankee Books.

There are plenty to thank and I'll begin with the players who gave me their time, shared a story or two about their contemporaries and supplied treasured photographs from their personal collections.

To the Red Sox publicity staff who granted me access to the locker room at Fenway Park or Chain O'Lakes Park in Winter Haven, Florida.

To Red Sox broadcaster Ken Coleman, a true pro.

To Bob Wood of Keene, New Hampshire, whose father was an early Red Sox star and an inspiration to anyone who was fortunate to meet him.

To Walter Cherniak of Plainville, Connecticut, and Scott Bushnell of St. Joe, Indiana, for their insights and immense knowledge of Red Sox history.

◆ FENWAY VOICES

To Carl Beane of Ware, Massachusetts, for his assistance and skills as an interviewer whom I have long admired.

To Red Sox fans everywhere. If you had stopped making the pilgrimage each summer to Fenway in the early 1950s, the Red Sox might have followed the Braves to another city.

Jack Lautier

Southington, Connecticut

1

Smoky Joe Wood

"S*moky" Joe Wood distinguished himself as a franchise pitcher in the early history of the Boston Red Sox. When healthy, Wood was as dominant as any of the great moundsmen of his era now in the Hall of Fame.*

Born Howard Ellsworth Wood, October 25, 1889, in Kansas City, Missouri, Smoky Joe reached the big leagues in 1908 and quickly established himself. In his second start, Wood tossed a one-hitter—the first of five he would register. Despite a variety of injuries in 1909 and 1910, Wood managed a combined 23-20 record. The following year, he won 23 games including a no-hitter over the St. Louis Browns on July 7.

In a sense, the tall right-hander was just warming up for 1912. It was that summer when Wood's achievements drew comparisons to Walter Johnson of Washington. As the season grew, so did the legend of Smoky Joe. At one point, he won 16 consecutive games to equal Johnson's American League mark during a sterling 34-5 season to propel the Red Sox to the pennant. Against the New York Giants in the World Series, Wood won three more games to help Boston to the championship.

That season, Wood and Johnson were among the league's best. Wood led in wins (34), winning percentage (.872), complete games (35) and shutouts (10). He finished second to Johnson in earned run average (1.39 to 1.91) and strikeouts (303 to 258). Always a champion of Johnson's abilities, Wood frequently maintained loyalty to his contemporaries. "If Walter had been on a team like the Red Sox, he would have set all kinds of records," said Wood.

Wood's banner campaign, however, may have taken its toll. In addition to working 344 innings, a shoulder injury in the spring of 1913 led to further arm trouble. Over the next three years, Smoky Joe won just 35 games and missed the entire 1916 season because of illness. While his lifetime totals—a 116-57 record and a 2.03 ERA—indicate a successful pitcher, Wood toiled only 1,434 innings.

The Red Sox eventually sold Wood to the Cleveland Indians for $15,000 on February 24, 1917. With the Tribe, Wood made only seven more appearances as a pitcher but found a second career as an outfielder. In six seasons, Wood batted .297 and helped the Indians to the championship in 1920.

Upon his retirement in 1922, Wood coached baseball at Yale University for 20 years. The institution eventually granted him an honorary doctorate—the first former baseball player to be so honored. Smoky Joe Wood was interviewed in 1982. He died July 29, 1985, in West Haven, Connecticut.

◆   ◆   ◆

There was nothing like being in there pitching. I wouldn't have traded my life in baseball for anything in the world. I would have given anything to have been a pitcher the whole time, to be on top rather than just another player. It's frustrating when you know you can't do it anymore because of pain. I was lucky I had something on the ball when I had it or they wouldn't have stayed with me as long as they did.

I always had a baseball in my hand, if I could get hold of one. Ever since I was big enough to throw a snowball, I wanted to play baseball. My life would not be worth living if it wasn't for baseball.

I never thought about becoming a big league baseball player because when I was a kid I didn't know there was a big league. I would have played for nothing if I could have made a living some other way. That's how much I thought of baseball.

I was ambitious as a kid. I worked more as a youngster than as a man. I was always finding ways to earn money. I guess I was a little like a scavenger. I collected scrap metal and looked in alleys for bottles to turn over a few cents. I even shined shoes.

I felt just fine as long as I was out there on the mound. I battled the Red Sox immediately over a contract. In fact, I went back to Ness City, Kansas, because they wouldn't pay me enough money. I think in those days $400 a month was considered quite a little. I wanted $600.

I guess I picked up some negotiating advice from my father. He was a lawyer, you know. Dad moved us to Chicago right after I was born to open a law practice. After about 10 years, he got the gold bug and headed for Alaska. But while he was there, he got what they called Yukon diarrhea and froze both legs so bad that he lost the feeling in them. He had to get out of there to save his life. They didn't fly people in there back then, so he wrapped gunny sacks around his legs and walked 30 miles a day.

It was against the Bloomer Girls in Ness City that I got my start in 1906. Ness City is about 60 miles north of Dodge City. I pitched for the town team, making six bucks a week and getting my meals. I really thought I was something. It was only amateur ball but that was the big thing in those days. Towards the end of the season the manager of the barnstorming Bloomer Girls came to me after a game. He said that if it was okay with my folks—I was 16 at the time—he would pay me $20 to spend the last three weeks with the team. I thought that was great. Baseball was the only thing that meant anything to me. I was tickled to death that I was able to go and play, once my father and mother said it was fine. So I went on the road and wound up in Wichita. I was the only one who needed transportation back home. When I returned, I found a young sister who had just been born.

My real start came the next year. A friend of my brother Harley, who was going to the University of Kansas, knew Belden Hill, who ran the Cedar Rapids team in the Three-I League. Belden offered me a contract for $90 a month, so before I knew what happened I was playing infield for Cedar Rapids.

During the winter, I received a letter from Belden saying that he had plenty of infielders and if I didn't mind, he would send my contract over to a friend who managed the Hutchinson club of the Western Association. Years later, Belden used to laugh about it and tell people that he gave away Joe Wood, which is exactly what he did.

I reported to the team and joined them on a southern trip. When all our pitchers came down with sore arms, they asked me if I could pitch. I said I would try. That was the last time I ever played the infield.

I had a pretty good year with Hutchinson. They sold me to Kansas City so I reported there next season. I pitched several innings against big league clubs coming up from the South. Word got around, I guess, that I was a good pitcher. My speed made an impression. They saw a pretty fair ballplayer in me. John I. Taylor was the president of the

Boston club and he sent Fred Lake, a scout, to take a look. The Red Sox bought me soon after that.

In Boston, the team made a big deal over me. They began looking for nicknames to call me, like "Ozone" or "Cyclone," but the one that stayed was the one Paul Shannon of the *Boston Post* gave me. I was pitching batting practice one day and Mr. Shannon said, "This kid certainly throws smoke." That's where "Smoky" came from. But I signed my name Joe Wood, not Smoky. Out of modesty, you know.

Cy Young was just finishing with the Red Sox. As I remember, the pitchers were Fred Burchell, Elmer Steele and Cy Morgan. The funny part of it is that our third baseman, Gavvy Cravath, made a big name for himself in the National League but he couldn't make it with us.

The best ballplayer I ever saw was Ty Cobb. I always said if there was a league higher than the majors, Ty Cobb would be the only fellow in it. Just as you'd be thinking about doing something, Ty would be doing it. When Cobb was on base, you knew he was going to go. He was always one step ahead. When I came up in 1908, all the catchers talked about was how Cobb could steal bases. They were saying, "I'll get him the next time."

When I pitched against Cobb, I voiced the same opinion as the catchers. All you could do was pray. It wasn't what you had, it was where he put it. Whatever you threw up there, he hit. Cobb had no trouble stealing second against me because I didn't have a good move to first base. Once he got to second, he had it a little tough. I didn't fear Cobb. Pete Compton of St. Louis was the guy who hit me like he owned my glove.

What I needed most as a pitcher was a receiver with a quick arm. Hick Cady was the fellow who really helped me. I couldn't hold a runner on base too well and Hick could really get something on the ball.

My big year in 1912, Cady caught most of my games. You know the Red Sox were ready to send him back to the bushes. I said to him one day, "Would you like to break in with me?" I broke in the catchers in my day. "I'd love it," he said.

I don't know how he got the nickname "Hick" but that's what the boys called him. He was an average player but he could certainly catch me. He was working like hell at trying to be a ballplayer.

The best ballplayer I ever knew was Tris Speaker. I might be a bit prejudiced because he and I were roommates for 15 years but there was no one in baseball like Spoke. You could see star written all over him. Spoke was one of the greatest players ever. He played a shallow center field, maybe 25 or 30 feet behind second base. It was in the day of the dead ball, but the ball wasn't that dead because there were home runs, though not many went over the fence.

We had a young pitcher in Boston who later became a great home run hitter. Babe Ruth was just a raw rookie in 1914. He used to come to me with questions all the time. I don't think you'd call it advice. He was just a big boy. There was no harm in him at all. Babe was a likeable guy.

In Boston and later in Cleveland, the fellow who really impressed me, especially when you needed a clutch hit, was Larry Gardner. I'm sure you've heard of Gardner. He won the last game of the 1912 Series for me with a fly ball. Larry could play third base with the best of them. I wouldn't trade him for five Frank Bakers.

I went to Cleveland as a pitcher but I couldn't do it anymore. My arm would hurt so much after pitching three or four innings, I couldn't play for a week. So they moved me to the outfield. It turned out to be a good break because I was able to play five more years.

Because of the war, the Indians were short of outfielders. Ed Miller was a decent first baseman but when he got hit in the chest trying to catch a fly ball, Braggo Roth came running in and said to Lee Fohl, the manager, "For gosh sakes, Lee. Put Woody out there. He'll catch the ball."

It took nothing to play the outfield. Catching a ball was easy. I had to work at becoming a better hitter. I choked up six or eight inches on the bat to get better balance. It takes a natural like Shoeless Joe Jackson to hold the bat at the end. When I was pitching, I held the bat that way. I tried to hit them a mile, like the boys do today, but now I had to hit to keep a job.

Baseball is a tough business, you know. Look at what happened to poor Ray Chapman. He was a wonderful fellow and in a flash, his life was over. Les Nunamaker and I carried him off the field that August day in 1920. Ray, to my knowledge, never regained consciousness.

As bad as I hate to say it, Carl Mays was a damn good pitcher. There was a story that Mays was going to get Chapman before the game but there was nothing to it. I don't know if Chapman was crossed up on the pitch. Stealing signs, you see, was an important part of the game in my day. I recall one time, Honus Wagner thought he had ours. He told Bobby Byrne I was going to throw a curve but I fired a bullet and hit him.

Baseball has not changed much except that the players have to play a little deeper in the outfield because of the lively ball. We had to catch the ball, too. Not like today when the glove catches the ball. There were no backhand stabs in my time because the ball didn't stay in the pocket. Today, the ball hits the glove, it stays there.

2

Jimmy Cooney

*J*immy *"Scoops" Cooney broke into professional baseball with the Boston Red Sox in 1917. It was one of seven seasons he would spend in the big leagues but the only year he played in the American League.*

"I'm 94 years old and the Red Sox are still my team," Cooney said in an interview in the fall of 1988.

Born August 24, 1894, in Cranston, Rhode Island, Cooney comes from a baseball family. His dad, Jimmy Sr., played for Cap Anson's Chicago Cubs in the early 1890s. His brother, Johnny, logged 20 years in the majors. He and his brother were teammates in 1928 on the Boston Braves.

"When I left baseball, I promoted softball. With all my relatives, we had a team with all Cooneys, 14 of us," says Jimmy. "Everywhere you looked, there was a Cooney."

From 1917 to 1928, Cooney appeared in 448 games in the majors. Besides both Boston teams, Cooney also played for the New York Giants, St. Louis Cardinals, Chicago Cubs and Philadelphia Phillies. Cooney's best season was 1924 when he batted .295 for the Cardinals.

Cooney was primarily a shortstop and was known for his fielding. He shares the National League record for most double plays (4) started in one game by a shortstop.

◆   ◆   ◆

I've always been a Red Sox fan, ever since I was a little kid. My family grew up in Cranston, and Fenway Park was less than an hour away by rail. I remember going to games to see Smoky Joe Wood pitch. He had good control for a fellow who threw mighty fast.

Boston was a great city to play in. The ballpark, for the most part, resembles the same field as when I played there. Well, Duffy's Cliff, that little knoll out in left field, is gone and they have the Wall now, but Fenway Park is baseball. Plenty of history, too.

One of my greatest days as a ballplayer was with the Red Sox in 1917. We were playing Washington and the boys were kidding me when I left the bench to bat against Walter Johnson. Everett Scott, our shortstop, remarked to me, "Cooney, you better start swinging now. This guy's pretty quick." That day, I got two hits, a single and a double. Not bad, for a rookie.

Smoky Joe Wood and Walter Johnson were the fastest pitchers I ever saw, but the guy who showed me as much stuff as anyone I batted against was Dazzy Vance. What a curve he had! He could really snap it off. Vance was the toughest pitcher I ever faced. He was a big guy, too.

The Red Sox were a powerhouse in the American League when I joined them. At the time, Babe Ruth was a pitcher and a darn good one. Babe was a good-natured fellow. The boys used to kid him all the time, calling him "Big Ape" or "Baboon," but Babe would always come back with a zinger himself. He knew his way around, you know.

I played four years in the minors before getting to the big leagues. In 1913, I played for Hall of Famer Jesse Burkett in Worcester. He was a tough old guy who had a quick temper. Boston bought my contract from Providence and when I reported to the big leagues, Jack Barry was the Red Sox manager. He also played second base. On the days he rested, I played. He didn't rest too much.

I wish I could have stayed in Boston for a longer time. I missed 1918 when the Red Sox won the World Series because I was in the Army. My regiment was ready to cross the Atlantic to fight the Kaiser but the armistice was signed. Everyone was glad the war was over. I was happy to get back to baseball. I missed the salary. We didn't make the kind of money they are paying the boys today. In those days, $500 a month was big money.

In 1919, the Red Sox sent me to Providence and the Grays later sold me to the New York Giants. I played a few games for John McGraw but I really wasn't much help to him. I came up with a sore arm in spring training the following year at San Antonio so McGraw shipped me to Milwaukee. I was with the Brewers in the American Association until 1924 when Branch Rickey cut a deal. That how I wound up with the St. Louis Cardinals.

Rickey was quite a character and a wonderful talker. He also knew baseball but he had a little luck, too.

One time, we were playing in Philadelphia and our starter was having a rough time. The Phillies, you know, were a good hitting team, especially at Baker Bowl. Rickey had Wee Willie Sherdel warming up in the bullpen, just in case things got out of hand. This particular day, Philadelphia loaded the bases with nobody out so Rickey decided to change pitchers. He brought in Sherdel who threw one pitch. Johnny Mokan was trying to bunt and he popped to Jim Bottomley at first. Sunny Jim threw the ball to me for the second out and I gunned a relay to Rogers Hornsby who covered first base to complete a triple killing. You should have seen Sherdel. He left the mound with his chest sticking out.

Let me tell you, a triple play is purely an accident. I've been involved in several and, not to brag, but I'm one of eight players in history to turn an unassisted triple play. Throughout my career, especially when I was in the field, the ball had a way of finding my glove.

It was Memorial Day in 1927 when I wound up in the record books. We were playing a morning game against Pittsburgh. In the fourth inning, the Bucs had runners on first and second. Tony Kaufmann was trying to pitch outside to Paul Waner. I was holding Lloyd Waner on second because he could run pretty good. Kaufmann got a pitch a bit too far in and Waner hit it back up the middle. It looked like the ball was going to go into center field but I speared it one-handed and stepped on second to double-up young Waner. Much to his surprise, Clyde Barnhart didn't know I had the ball until I tagged him out sliding into second. Joe McCarthy came running out on the field to shake my hand.

Believe it or not, the very next day, Johnny Neun, a first baseman with Detroit, did the same thing against Cleveland. Talk about coincidences! I was happy to finally pay back Pittsburgh. In 1925, Glenn Wright, their great shortstop, had pulled the identical one-man show against us. I was on second and Rogers Hornsby was on first when Wright gloved Bottomley's smash and got us all out.

With the Cardinals, I played alongside one of the game's great hitters. Hornsby was gifted with a bat in his hands, no question about it. However, he also had a little help. Jim Gould was president of the

Baseball Writers and on any questionable play, where maybe one of the infielders muffed the ball a little, Hornsby got a hit. That kind of leverage only helps your average.

To his credit, Hornsby took great care of himself. He didn't go to movies because the light would hurt his eyes. Hornsby could run like hell and had quite a record as a bunter, too. I recall one series against the Giants where he got five hits—all bunts!

Hornsby liked to play cards, especially poker. On an off day, he'd invite the boys over to his house. He asked me two or three times to go but I never did. With his vision, I figured he could see right through my cards.

Hornsby was a hitter but Shoeless Joe Jackson was the best natural I ever looked at. Every move he made was perfect. However, neither compared to Ty Cobb. He was the best hitter I ever saw.

I didn't get to play against Cobb that long but he must have been something. I remember one game in Detroit where the fans booed him something bad. Cobb dropped his bat at home plate, walked over to the noise and challenged the fans behind the Tiger bench. *"I'll fight any son of a BEE here,"* he yelled. No one came forward.

Cobb was always ready to fight. He had some trouble with one of the Boston writers. I believe it was Paul Shannon. One day, Cobb beat out a hit down the third base line. Shannon, however, gave Larry Gardner an error and that took the hit away. The next day, Cobb came out early and hollered a whole string of bad names at Shannon over the misdeed.

I went to the Cubs for pitcher Vic Keen in 1926. Joe McCarthy was there, a great manager. He was easy to understand and he'd help you if you had a problem. In those days, we didn't have the number of coaches like they have today. We didn't get much coaching because they expected you to do a job. When you couldn't do it, they had plenty of others who could take yours.

Sparky Adams was my roommate in Chicago. The Cubs trained on Catalina Island off California and one time, just before noon, Sparky and I played a little trick on Gabby Hartnett. He and Guy Bush were having lunch, so Sparky and I went around, gathered all the furniture we could move and packed it into Hartnett's room. We did it so Gabby could just about open his door. Boy, was he sore, especially at me since I was from the same state as he was.

Hartnett was a great catcher. What a beautiful throwing arm! His ball was light to handle at second base.

Because of baseball, I got to see the country. I trained all over the place—in Florida, California, even in Texas. In 1924, I went to Cuba and batted .390 down there. Our manager was a fellow named Acosta. His father was sort of the mayor of Marianao, the town we played in. He always wore a gun. The umpire hardly ever made a decision against our club.

The boys called me "Scoops" because of my fielding. That came natural to me. My batting average in the majors was .262 which is a little better than medium but I was not the hitter my brother Johnny was. He batted over .300 eight times during his career. I hit .350 in Buffalo one year, but that wasn't the majors.

Johnny and I were teammates briefly when I came back to Boston and played with the Braves. Over the years, we battled each other several times. One time, he drilled me in the ribs with a pitch. Johnny originally came up as a pitcher and became an outfielder because of an injury. He spent close to two decades in the bigs as a player and later as a coach. My younger brother was just amazing.

3

John
Michaels

*I*t may have been the darkest summer in club history but to a 22-year-
old rookie named John Michaels, it was his proud moment in the
big leagues.

Among the perennial distant finishes by the Red Sox in the
1920s and early 1930s, the toughest year for even the most loyal of Red
Sox rooters must have been 1932, when the Red Hose anchored 64 games
out of first place. A paltry 182,150 ventured to Fenway Park that season
as the franchise dropped to its all-time depth— 43 wins and 111 defeats.

But for Michaels, a southpaw with a good curveball, regardless of how
sad the Red Sox were that season, it remains his one year of "glory" in the
majors.

Born in Bridgeport, Connecticut, on July 10, 1907, Michaels developed
his baseball skills as a high school pitcher. After some success in the
minors, Michaels made the big leagues. With the Red Sox, he appeared
in 28 games, beating the pennant-winning Yankees for his only victory
among seven decisions.

◆ FENWAY VOICES

While an arm injury curtailed his career and made his tenure in Boston just a footnote, Michaels will be allied forever with one of the game's most devastating forces. On the afternoon of September 24, 1932, Michaels was on the mound when Babe Ruth slugged his 652nd lifetime home run, his final blast that summer.

◆   ◆   ◆

You look up Babe Ruth's record and somewhere you'll see my name next to his. It was late in the season, our last home game. Marty McManus had put me in the game just to save a pitcher who was to start the next day.

We were behind 7-2 in the ninth. Ruth's the first man up. We didn't draw too well all season but the people in the park that day were cheering for Ruth, knowing it would be his final appearance in Boston. I think they were hoping Babe would hit a home run.

Benny Tate, our catcher, called for a fastball but I shook him off. He called for another one, but again I shook him off. He asked for time and came out to the mound.

"Hey, John," he says. "Don't you want to throw a fastball?"

Tate, like everyone else, knew my fastball, on a good day, wasn't fast at all. I was a curveball pitcher. Had a darn good one, too.

So Tate again starts telling me what pitch I should throw to Ruth.

"John, the game is lost. You're not the losing pitcher. Let's see how far this big fellow can hit one."

From where I stood, I had a darn good vantage point. I threw him a fastball, belt high. Babe hit it good. He could hit a ball as high as he could hit one long. This ball must've had snow on it. Landed halfway up the right-field bleachers. And all the people clapped and cheered.

The year I played for the Red Sox, we were in the cellar and most of the games didn't mean much. I recall a game Paul Andrews was pitching. I was sitting on the bench and McManus says, "Gee, I hope he lays one in there." Well, Andrews threw four wide ones to Ruth and the people booed the hell out of him.

When he came in the dugout, McManus asked him why he walked Ruth instead of letting him hit one.

"If I gave him a home run, it would start a rally," Andrews said.

By walking him, I said to myself, he also can start a rally.

That tells you something about the team in those days. My salary for the whole year was $2,750. Bob Quinn sent me a contract before spring training in 1932, but I sent it back. I had a good year in Triple A and figured I was worth more money. Quinn called me and wanted to know why I sent him my contract without signing it. "I thought I was in the big leagues," is what I told him.

I won only one game in the big leagues and my only strikeout that day was Babe Ruth. I threw a curve, right over the center of the plate on a three-and-two pitch. Babe threw his bat and started trotting down to first base but Owens, the umpire, said, "Strike three." Babe complained a bit but I think Owens gave me a break. It was my first year in the league. Some people didn't think much of Owens as an umpire, but that day I thought he was the best.

But don't let anyone kid you. Babe Ruth was the greatest player in baseball. I remember an exhibition game he played against us in Albany one year. He came into our clubhouse and joined the rest of us, drinking beer and eating hot dogs. Besides hitting home runs, I think that's all that he ever did.

In those days, baseball was a carnival and I was just happy to be in the big leagues. The first major league game I ever saw was in Washington on Opening Day in '32 and President Hoover threw out the first ball. But if it wasn't for my brother-in-law, I probably would never have made it.

I pitched for Warren Harding High in Bridgeport. Not to brag, but I could throw pretty good. Few could hit my drop or curveball. My best game was a no-run, no-hit game against Wilby, a school in Waterbury.

There was an Eastern League team in Hartford and one day I get this letter in the mail from Paddy O'Connor telling me to report for a tryout. All I'm thinking is "Who told him about me?"

My brother-in-law was a big baseball fan. I told him about the letter and was thinking about not going because O'Connor explained that his club would not cover my expenses and I didn't have the money to go up there. My brother-in-law told me not to worry. On the ride to Hartford, he explained he had taken some clippings and wrote a letter to O'Connor about this left-handed pitcher.

I worked out at Bulkeley Stadium and O'Connor liked what he saw. "We'll give you a contract for $150 a month," he said. It doesn't sound like a lot, but in those days it was pretty good money.

My parents were from the old country, Czechoslovakia. My real last name is Maco but my father changed it. He was a saloon keeper right across from the ballpark in Bridgeport. I could sit up in the windows and watch all the games when I was a kid. He didn't mind me going away. My mother always cried when I left for spring training. I was her baby, the youngest of 11 kids.

I felt I could play baseball and I figured my chances of making a second division team were better than, say, the Yankees. I wonder how many pitchers didn't get a chance with guys like Gomez, Ruffing and Pennock ahead of them. Our best pitcher in Boston was Danny

MacFayden and he couldn't even get regular work when he went to New York later that season.

When I joined the Red Sox, they were a cellar team. We had some talented players but not enough. Earl Webb set a record for doubles one year and they traded him. Wilcy Moore was a good relief pitcher and they sent him away. The Red Sox were always making trades because Quinn had money trouble. He would make deals for Smead Jolley and Dale Alexander but he'd sell someone else within a week. We just didn't draw the people in. One time we played a doubleheader against St. Louis and there may have been 250 people in the ballpark. We were in last place and they were next to last.

When Quinn made the trades for Alexander, Jolley and Roy Johnson, we were finally able to score some runs. The first game I ever started for the Red Sox was in a doubleheader against Philadelphia. MacFayden, who was our stopper, was going to pitch the first game and I was going to pitch the second. The Athletics were going with Earnshaw and Mahaffey. Shano Collins, who began the season as our manager, figured we couldn't beat Earnshaw so MacFayden would pitch against Mahaffey.

In the first inning, we got two men on against Earnshaw and Jolley hits a home run. I'm saying to myself that's all I need. Well, the first guy up was Max Bishop. He walked a lot that season and I helped him. I threw him four straight balls. Then I walked Mule Haas. Mickey Cochrane was next. I got one strike but I ended up walking him too. Three batters, all left-handers, and I walked them.

Shano took me out before I walked any more and brought in Bob Weiland, another lefty. Foxx is the first guy up and he hit a line drive over third to score two runs. Shano took Weiland out and he brought in Bob Kline to face Al Simmons. Simmons hit a line drive over the short-stop's head and two more runs scored. Two of us were in the shower and Philadelphia had already outscored us in the first inning. Weiland was laughing but I was worried. I felt terrible about it. Later on, Shano asked me if I was afraid out on the mound. "If you can't get a left-handed hitter out, you're no good to my ballclub." What could I say? Shano was right.

My best game in the big leagues was the day I beat the Yankees for my only win. I beat Ruffing, but I was lucky. I didn't allow a base hit to either Ruth, Gehrig or Lazzeri and they were due to come up if Marv Olson didn't make a good play on a ball hit by Joe Sewell. The Yankees had scored twice in the ninth to make it 6-5 and had the bases loaded. Sewell was a left-handed hitter and he had gotten two hits already off of me. He hit a hard ground ball to second base. Olson got down on both knees and saved the game for me.

I hurt my arm during the season and it was never the same. I never

16

made it back to the majors although the White Sox were interested in me. The Red Sox turned it around when Mr. Yawkey bought the ballclub, but I wasn't there to see it. They started to get pitchers like Lefty Grove and Wes Ferrell and hitters like Jimmy Foxx and Ted Williams. We could have used a few more like them when I was playing.

4

Bobby Doerr

*I*n 1988, Hall of Famer Bobby Doerr, who wore No. 1, became the third player in Boston Red Sox history to have his uniform numeral retired. It only seemed fitting since, in fan voting in 1969 and 1982 to determine the franchise's all-time players, Doerr was the overwhelming choice at second base.

With the exception of his rookie year and a military hitch in 1945, Doerr was Boston's regular second baseman from 1938 to 1951. It became an annual rite that Doerr would either lead the American League in fielding or share the distinction. In 1948, he compiled a streak of 414 chances, covering nearly three months, without an error. At the plate, Doerr had a .288 lifetime batting average with six seasons of 100 or more runs batted in.

Born in Los Angeles on April 7, 1918, Doerr signed with the Red Sox after three outstanding years in the Pacific Coast League. During his 14-year career with Boston, Doerr collected 2,042 hits including 223 home runs. In 1943, it was Doerr's three-run homer which won the first All-Star

Game played at night. The following year, he was voted the league's MVP by The Sporting News *after batting a career-high .325 and leading the league with a .528 slugging percentage. In his only World Series appearance, Doerr batted .409 in 1946, tops among Boston regulars. His best season at the plate was 1950 when, at age 32, Doerr led the league in triples, scored 103 runs, garnered 120 runs batted in and slugged 27 home runs.*

◆   ◆   ◆

Back in the 1920s when I was growing up, there really wasn't that much in the way of major sports in California. The Chicago Cubs had spring training on Catalina Island but we didn't see that much big-league baseball. It was quite a thrill to go down to Wrigley Field in Los Angeles and watch an exhibition game. I'll always remember as a little kid seeing all those bats and wondering how I could get my hands on one of them.

I can remember, as a young boy, maybe 12 or 13, throwing a tennis ball against the porch steps by the hour. I look back and realize it was a lot of help. There's a certain rhythm you create doing that, just like catching an egg. You watch an Ozzie Smith or some of the other good infielders, they have their hands out in front of them, ready to suck up the ground balls. You learn that from constant practice.

That's what worked for myself and Johnny Pesky. We would practice and practice. The biggest thing is knowing how the other fellow is going to handle the ball. You play alongside of each other, you get used to playing and anticipating and knowing where your partner is going to be, his habits and things. The longer you're around the league also helps because you know the hitters and how a pitcher is going to work certain hitters. A real break in my early days was playing alongside Joe Cronin. He knew all the players, what pitch to expect from a pitcher and where you should be positioned in the field.

In those days, everything was not such a fast-paced existence. Things didn't change so much. Today, a computer can be the top of the line but it has to be remodeled next year because what it can do is outdated. That's the way life is today. The media puts more pressure on players today, too. People want to know more about the players and television has taken pro sports into everyone's living room. The pressure is tenfold. In my time, the top players had to face constant pressure but today, everyone faces it because of TV. People see these players like they are movie actors. Before, you were just a ballplayer.

Here's a good example of how much things have changed. In 1946, we took the radio rights from the World Series to help get the baseball pension system started. The way it was set up back then was this way. If a player had 10 years of service at age 50, he would get $100 a month for the rest of his life. If he had five years of service, he'd get $50. If he played six years, he'd get $60 and so forth. At the time, I had played 10 years and boy, I thought, wasn't that something to have $100 a month coming at age 50. Now, because of television, the pension is up to $90,000 a year. Back then, $100 seemed great. Today, you might have just enough to pay your electric bill for a month.

Living in southern California, the two teams in the area were the Hollywood Stars and the Los Angeles Angels. The Angels were owned by the Cubs, but most clubs were independents like the Stars. I broke in with them when I was 16 years old.

George Myatt and I were the middle infield combination. He played shortstop and was a couple of years older than I. One scout, covering the West Coast for the Red Sox, had recommended us to Boston. Eddie Collins came out in 1935, liked what he saw and took out an option on the two of us. A year later, Collins returned to decide if he was going to buy our contracts. Joe Cronin was still playing shortstop so the Red Sox decided to take me.

At that same time, Ted Williams had just signed with the San Diego team. One day, Collins was watching him take batting practice. He liked Ted so much, that he made arrangements that the Red Sox would get first chance at signing Teddy the following year. That was quite a thing to see. Collins and Bill Lane of the San Diego club agreed on a handshake.

The Coast League was a good league but it was a big adjustment for a young player. There were a number of veterans who helped your confidence when things went a little tough. The older fellows, like Cedric Durst, were good advisors but you had to ask for help because that's the way it was when they grew up. Sometimes if you wanted to find something out, you would go to a player on a different club. He might give you a little tip or two.

I had a real good year in the Coast League in 1936 and I kind of think, if I had come up in late September and maybe played in a few games or so, I would have been adjusted to what to expect the next year. In '37, everything was new. I didn't play all that much as a rookie. But looking back, it was great the way things worked out. That fall, I went up to Oregon to fish and that's where I met my wife. She was a schoolteacher in Oregon and my whole life changed. We have a home in Agness, a town on the Rogue River. I'm from the city but I just love that country. Things are meant to be.

One of the biggest things I found in the big leagues was that every day, you'd see a good pitcher and good, good fielders. The defense would take quite a few hits away, just like a good pitcher would. I recall going into Yankee Stadium and facing Lefty Gomez, Bump Hadley and Monte Pearson. They were real good pitchers and it was a bit tough. I was only 19 years old and overwhelmed a bit going into a game and playing against a Lou Gehrig. At the time, I was concerned about it because if this was what the majors were all about, it wasn't going to be easy.

One team that made it look easy was the Yankees. They were a well-balanced ballclub with disciplined players. The Yankees always had a good relief pitcher, a specialist which was unusual in those days, a Johnny Murphy, a Joe Page. Look at '48, '49 and '50, we did have Ellis Kinder, but "Old Folks" was also starting games for us. The Yankees always had the starters to go with a reliever. If we had been fortunate to have had one good reliever, we probably would have won more pennants.

Take the '46 season. We had good pitching all year. Tex Hughson wins 20. Dave Ferriss wins 25. Mickey Harris wins 17. We broke to an early lead and maybe lost 16 games all season at Fenway Park. The next year, our big three came down with sore arms. When you have the pitching to go with good hitting and defense, you'll find a way to win.

As for hitting, I'm sure you could fill a few notebooks if I start talking about Ted Williams. He was so sharp, so much sharper than the other players. They say he was gifted with a lot of talent, but some of the things he did with a bat, well, it wasn't an accident that he hit .406 in '41. Ted was the first to go to light bats. In those days, the bats were 35 ounces and 35 inches and Ted was the first to go to a 32- or 33-ounce bat. I remember Ted going to Mr. Hillerich of the Louisville Slugger Company and wanting to get lighter bats. He felt a hitter wouldn't get good wood on the ball using a heavier bat. Ted wanted one that he could handle and get the joy part of on the ball. Ted was strong enough to swing a heavier bat but he wanted to control it. One time, he got a dozen bats in and there was something wrong with them. At the factory, the worker on the lathe took too much off the handle, just a fraction of an inch but Ted could tell if a bat weighed 33 or 34 ounces. He kept postal scales in the clubhouse to weigh bats. That's how sharp he was. Ted would always do exercises to keep his arms strong. He'd watch pitchers warm up before a game and then take a pitch the first time at bat to see if that pitcher was a little quicker today than from the last time he saw him. It was more than just ability; Ted was just ahead of everybody else.

Teddy started that bit about me as captain of the Red Sox. When you're in the infield, you are sort of in the play all the time. And as one of the older players, you just sort of assume some type of leadership. I was never officially designated as captain but Teddy said things like "Captain Bobby Doerr" and it stuck.

They tell me I'm one of a handful or so of second basemen in history to have hit over 200 home runs but I don't pay close attention to that stuff. I suppose not many middle infielders hit with power but the surprising thing is that Tony Lazzeri and Charlie Gehringer are the only second basemen to have driven in over 100 runs in seven different seasons. I did that six times. Rogers Hornsby did it five times, which I figure, the way he hit, he'd have a whole bunch more than me.

For a long time, the emphasis was on the power hitters to be considered for the Hall of Fame. Little consideration was given to middle infielders or defensive players. Very seldom do you have a shortstop or a second baseman who hits .300, drives in 100 or more runs and hits 20 or 30 home runs. When they put in a couple of guys like Lou Boudreau, Pee Wee Reese and Luis Aparicio, I felt I might have a chance. I came real close a couple of times. When the phone rang about nine o'clock in the morning, and it was Ed Stack of the Hall of Fame Committee, as soon as he said his name, I knew I was going to Cooperstown. It was just a great thrill. My phone rang the rest of the day and it topped everything I've ever done in baseball.

5

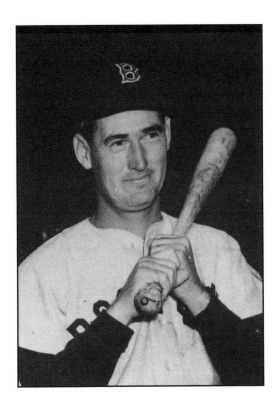

Ted
Williams

Voted the "Greatest Red Sox Player Ever" in a poll by Boston rooters in 1982 and named to the starting outfield in a national vote of baseball fans who picked the game's "Greatest Living Team" in 1969, Hall of Famer Theodore Samuel Williams was the focus of the Boston franchise for four decades.

Arguably the game's premier hitter despite having his career twice herniated by stints in the military service, from 1939 until his Fenway farewell—his 521st lifetime homer in a dramatic last at-bat against Baltimore's Jack Fisher on September 28, 1960—Williams rewrote the major league record book. A model emulated by peers and future players alike, Williams batted a composite .344 over 19 seasons, won six batting titles, two Triple Crowns, appeared in 18 All-Star Games, drove in and scored over 100 runs 10 different seasons and won two Most Valuable Player Awards. He was also the last player to log a .400 season—batting .406 in 1941 which is the highest since Rogers Hornsby hit .424 in 1924.

A master of hitting, one of the world's most respected fishermen and

*among the best ever to pilot a fighter plane, Williams could and did it all.
An individualist, sometimes moody, sometimes gentle, there is another
side of Williams which is revered by friends and teammates but unknown
to many, especially his critics.*

*Baseball fans love to estimate the type of statistics Williams would
have produced if he did not miss five summers because of the military, yet
it is **what Williams did** when he played that makes one wonder how
pitchers were able to get him out! Maybe that's why many decided to walk
him 2,019 times—a stretch that is equivalent to four full seasons.*

◆　　　◆　　　◆

It is easy to criticize the modern ballplayer. I was playing in Minneapolis in 1938 and Rogers Hornsby, the greatest right-handed hitter
who ever lived, was an old coach with the Millers. He was only 45 then
and I was a young player trying to listen to every word he said. Now
Hornsby was an outspoken guy but he taught me a lot about hitting, like
what makes a good hitter, or how a hitter must make adjustments for
all situations—the count, the pitcher from the last ballgame.

That year, there was a young fellow in New York who had a tremendous season. Joe DiMaggio led the league in everything and was holding
out for $25,000. All I remember is Hornsby saying, "I wonder who the
hell he thinks he is?"

I played against Joe DiMaggio longer than any player and he was
the greatest player I ever saw. In fact, I played with or against the entire
family. Dom and I were teammates in Boston. Vince and I were together
in the Coast League.

My great advantage in life was being born in California, living a
block-and-a-half from the playground and being able to play baseball 11
or 12 months a year. Just being able to hit, hit, hit, hit. Hitting a
baseball is the hardest thing to do in sports. It still is. You have to play
as much as you can, put in as many hours as you can, dedicate yourself
to reach the final product. You must have some talent but to succeed, you
need the opportunity. My kid would love to be a baseball player but he
lives in Vermont on a hill and there is no one to play with. Heck, the
high school team might play 15 games a season. In San Diego, we played
sandlot ball every night and that was a great, great help.

I joined the San Diego club in the Coast League in 1936 when I was
17 years old. In those days, the major league teams would buy players
from the minor league teams or work a deal with a club owner to get the
rights to a prospect, like an option to buy a piece of lakefront property.

On our first road trip, we were up in Portland. The Red Sox had an
option to buy Bobby Doerr, and Eddie Collins, the general manager, had

come out to Oregon to either drop the option or pick it up. But while Mr. Collins was deciding for sure to sign Bobby, he saw me hit in batting practice, which was the only regular work for me that season. I couldn't even swing I was so tight. I pinch-hit once and took three strikes right down the middle.

"Who's that young outfielder out there?" Mr. Collins asked Bill Lane, who owned the ballclub.

Mr. Lane didn't know who Mr. Collins was talking about.

"The young, left-hand hitting outfielder?"

And Mr. Lane still didn't know who Mr. Collins was talking about.

"The young kid you just signed?"

"Oh that kid. He hasn't played yet. Heck, he's three or four years away."

"What's his name?"

"Williams."

"Just give me the first option on him."

Now, Mr. Collins, a great tribute to him as a baseball man, immediately felt, through the brawn and natural ability, that I had a chance to be a good hitter. I hardly played that season but sure enough, the next year, Mr. Collins picked up the option on me and I became property of the Red Sox.

When I think of the Red Sox, the memory of Tom Yawkey is always with me. His name will always mean kindness, a leader in a quiet way, a very humble man. He wanted to do the best he could for everybody. I really believe that. He was not a complicated person. He was great to me and I treasured our friendship.

When Mr. Yawkey was a young man, 33 or 34, he used to spend a month-and-a-half in the Great Divide in Wyoming. He'd invite people like Eddie Collins, Ty Cobb, Jimmy Foxx, Mike Higgins and Lefty Grove. Mr. Yawkey wanted to be with his people in a different way. He knew them as players during the summer but he also knew they all liked to hunt. I was unlucky because I got to Boston a little too late.

In my day, they'd have those big pheasant hunts in Sioux City but I never went to any of them because I loved to hunt mallards. My greatest joy is to be out there alone. Put out 18 or so jumbo decoys. Get a little lumbercraft, camouflage it with a bale of hay in the brush and stuff, set the blind up just right and wait by the hour for a little bunch to come in there. I could do that so easy. I had the patience of Job. I really loved to do that. I like the beauty of the country and that's why I fish. Make your next cast a little smoother, a little better than the last one. I love the expectations of "UMMM. . .there he is by gosh!" You can cast 500 times a day expecting a hit on the line. It might only happen three times in a day but the chance is there all the time.

The first time I went fishing, I caught some bass. From there, I tried the surf in San Diego with a wonderful man, Mr. Cassie. I played on the same team with his son, but Mr. Cassie's kid didn't care anything about fishing so he'd take me along. For companionship, I guess. Heck, surf casting was great fun. After a while I was able to cast as far as anybody on the beach. We'd catch the tide, wade in almost to our waists and get soaking wet.

Cold weather always bothered me a little bit. But the funny part of it is, when I played in the Midwest, which is Minneapolis, Indianapolis, Toledo and Columbus, all of those towns in there, that was the hottest weather I had ever seen. It's tremendously hot in the summer but it's too cold in the winter.

The heat didn't bother me as much as the cold. Early spring and late fall, I'll tell you, it bothered me. I was never comfortable playing, and I don't think anyone really is, although there were some guys who thrive in cold weather. The way they have opened up things today, I think it would be even harder to hit .400 because the season is a week longer in the spring and ends a little later, too.

I'm not a very religious person but I feel I've been God-blessed as much as anyone I know. I've been lucky. I've gone through different instances of life that I wouldn't want to go through again, but I don't want to go back one day. I might have lost a leg yesterday if I had to do it over again. I know the closeness I've come at times to getting wiped out but I know I'll feel better tomorrow. It will be a better day. Who knows. I might strike oil. I want to keep going ahead. See my kid get an A in French.

6

Charlie "Broadway" Wagner

*T*he players called him "Broadway" for the stylish way he dressed. But on the mound, especially wearing the Red Sox jersey, Charlie Wagner proved to be yeomanly...until his career was interrupted by World War II.

After brief trials with the Red Hose from 1938 to 1940, the right-hander posted a combined 26-19 mark over the next two seasons, including a career-best 14-11 in 1942. In October of that year, Wagner enlisted in the U.S. Navy and did not return to baseball until the war was over.

After returning to the Red Sox, Wagner pitched in only eight games for the pennant-winners in 1946 to conclude a composite major league career with 100 appearances, a 32-23 record and a 3.91 earned run average. Upon retirement, Wagner moved into the front office and served as Boston's assistant farm director from 1947 to 1960. In later years, Wagner has worked in other capacities, ranging from scout to coach to roving instructor in the minor leagues.

◆   ◆   ◆

Some of the younger players today don't realize it, but every ballplayer gets old. I've been associated with this great game for over 50 years. They said baseball wouldn't last but it has. And for me, it has been 50 beautiful years.

I was born in Reading, Pennsylvania, in 1912. One thing we had in Reading was professional baseball. As a kid, you always aped somebody. My idol was Ted Lyons. I'd go to the Phillies games just to see him play. That whole process came into being for me. There were others to emulate too. Later on, everyone wanted to be a Ted Williams and rightfully so. You pick a guy who's going to be great, a can't-miss.

I'm not sure we missed anything growing up in our time. Back then, most families simply didn't have the money to travel around. Some did take the train to Atlantic City but that took a whole day to do, to go a distance of 100 or so miles. In those days, life, too, was more home-oriented. Not everyone had a car. The cars didn't go fast and the highway system wasn't like it is today. Now, everyone seems to be able to get on a plane and go anywhere. People stuck around and painted the house or something.

To tell you the truth, you really didn't know how poor you were. You just kept going and going until times turned around. You didn't realize just how small your salary was because the price of everything was relative. A loaf of bread was five cents. My first year in professional baseball, I was paid $100 a month but I was able to save money. We received three dollars and seventy-five cents in meal money from the ballclub but you could get a full-course dinner for a dollar sixty-five.

Looking back, as the country grew up, so did baseball and myself along with it. I was a batboy for Reading in the International League. Some of the great ones came through there. And the nostalgia part of it, when I graduated to the majors, these fellows were still playing in the big leagues. To come up to the big show and see my guys, the Moe Bergs, the Heinie Schubles. It was simply beautiful.

Years ago, baseball didn't have many scouts and they were not knocking on everyone's door. We had the Red Sox affiliate in Reading for a period. One of the players on the team was Lefty Hockette who later pitched in Boston. I was pitching batting practice one day and Nemo Leibold, the manager, asked "Would you like a tryout?" That's how it started. The next year, 1935, I was assigned to Charlotte and began my professional career in the Piedmont League.

Before I reached the big leagues, I had to learn how to pitch. My first year, I went 7-and-16. The next year at Rocky Mount, I won 20 games. I won 20 again the next season at Minneapolis. That was the way the calling order went back then. You had to earn a right to be considered. The kids today have great talent but the game, at the big league level, is something like on-the-job training. Some young kid wins five games in a row in Triple A and he gets the call. I'm not saying the pitchers today don't have strong arms but they lack that little extra experience of pitching in situations.

Try and guess the number of times a pitcher over the course of a season faces a first-and-third, no-out situation? Or maybe runners on second-and-third and one out? You have to build up confidence and the minor leagues are terrific for that. Someone shouldn't be annoyed at spending a year or two more in the minors because it pays off in the end. When you get to the show, you'll stay there.

In the big leagues, I was called "Broadway" by the players because I had a flashy taste for clothes. I liked to dress up. In my day, all the players wore ties. Well, almost everyone. Ted Williams had nice clothes but he never wore a tie. When he did, Ted knew where he could get one. "How in the world do you tie this?" he'd moan. A couple of years back when the Red Sox had a big dinner for me, Ted made sure he reminded everybody what he was wearing. In his speech, Ted said, "I have to tell Wagner one thing. The minute this night is over, I'm going to give him his tie back."

Like many others, I had a hitch in World War II and spent time with the U.S. Navy in Australia and in the Philippines. Where I was stationed, it wasn't real combat, more like being jostled from this installation to the next one. I was glad to see the war end. I couldn't wait to get my hands on a baseball.

Back in the States, there was a fervor for baseball, a tempo you just couldn't believe. The '46 Red Sox grew up in that tempo. It was fascinating. Upbeat. Let's go. A team effort. That attitude helped us win the pennant. The Red Sox certainly had the players with Williams and Pesky and the pitching on that club.

I wish I could have contributed more. When I returned from the war, I came back with some form of dysentery but the Boston club was nice enough to keep me around for the whole season. I was getting near that age where I could have gone on for a couple of seasons but the Red Sox offered me a chance to join their organization. In my mind, I felt I could still pitch but that first year out of the service was a little rough to get reorganized. Many of the players came back. Others lost it because of age or wounds. The younger guys were able to recoup.

I had an opportunity to play alongside the great ones in baseball. Not good ones—*Great* ones. Go right down the list. Start it with DiMaggio, Greenberg, York, Foxx, Williams, Cronin, Averill. You don't get any better. That distinguishes itself. All of those things go into the game because, even on my day off, I enjoyed watching baseball. The only problem was the day you had to pitch. There were too many great hitters to get out.

7

Johnny Pesky

*J*ohnny Pesky started as a clubhouse boy and ran errands for the
Pacific Coast League team in his native Portland, Oregon. These
modest beginnings launched what would evolve into a 10-year
major league playing career followed by managing, coaching and
broadcasting. Today, Pesky is a special assistant to the general manager
of the Boston Red Sox.

A lifetime .307 hitter, Pesky is remembered by many for a play in Game
7 of the 1946 World Series against St. Louis. The daring Enos Slaughter,
going on the pitch, scored from first base on a hit by Harry Walker in the
last of the eighth to give the Cardinals a 4-3 victory. Critics say Pesky was
guilty of holding the relay toss from outfielder Leon Culberson, a reserve
who was not noted for a strong throwing arm. At the same time, observers
have forgotten that the Bosox stranded the tying and go-ahead runs on base
in the ninth and never solved the pitching of Harry Brecheen, the Series
Most Valuable Player. The Cardinal southpaw became the first pitcher
since Stan Coveleski in 1920 to win three games in the Fall Classic.

◆ FENWAY VOICES

Born John Paveskovich on September 27, 1919, Pesky's ability to hit drew the attention of scouts in high school. He signed with the Red Sox and quickly developed into a leadoff man. Primarily a singles hitter, Pesky batted .325 at Rocky Mount in the Piedmont League in 1940. A year later, he again batted .325 at Louisville of the American Association.

Once in Boston, Pesky combined with Dominic DiMaggio as "table-setters" for Ted Williams. In 1942, as a rookie, Pesky led the majors in hits (205) en route to a .331 season. Though a three-year hitch in the Navy interrupted his career, Pesky came back to again lead the American League in hits (208) in 1946 and in 1947 (207) and thus equaled a major league record by collecting at least 200 hits in his first three years in the big leagues. Each season, Pesky finished third in the batting race. On May 8, 1946, in a 14-10 win over Chicago, Pesky became the first AL player to score six runs in a game.

A competent gloveman at three infield positions, Pesky also played for Detroit and Washington. He batted over .300 six times with the Bosox before moving to the Tigers on June 4, 1952 in a nine-player deal that brought George Kell and Dizzy Trout to Fenway. After 192 games with the Tigers over three years, Pesky went to the Senators on June 14, 1954, in a trade for Mel Hoderlein.

Pesky began his managerial career in 1956. He made several stops in the minors before taking the helm in Boston. He won titles at Lancaster, Pennsylvania, in 1958 and at Knoxville in 1959. With the Red Sox, Pesky had a combined 147-178 record in 1963, 1964 and briefly in 1980.

◆   ◆   ◆

In 1944, I became a commissioned officer in the Navy and my father was amazed at how quickly I had risen in the ranks.

"Johnny, do you know how long it would take you to become an officer in my country?"

"Pa, let me tell you something," I said. "In the first place, there's a war on. Secondly, we're not in your country and third, the government can have my gold bar if I can go back to playing baseball." To this day, I have never lost my enthusiasm for baseball. I never will. I always thought if I wanted to do anything in sports, baseball seemed to offer a longer and better life. In our day, we played the game because we got jobs out of it.

As a kid, I worked for the Portland team shining shoes and washing towels when Red Berger, Pinky Higgins, Ben Stankey, Johnny Morrow, Jim Kiesel, John Frederick, Earl Grecker and Bill Kronan played there. My family lived four blocks from the ballpark.

Being that close to baseball, I knew what I wanted to do. There is nothing like putting on a uniform. What helped me early in my career was having a high school coach who, I don't like to use the word, was demanding. He'd come in and say "This is what you have to do to win." I had great admiration and respect for him and his philosophy has stayed with me.

Scouts were always at my games but the reason I signed with Boston was Ernie Johnson. I actually got higher offers from other teams but my mother really liked Mr. Johnson. He would sit in the kitchen and have coffee with my folks. He would always bring flowers for my mother and some bourbon for my father.

I was one of 55 ballplayers in training camp trying to win a job with Rocky Mount, a Class B team in the Piedmont League. I thought I'd be going to C ball but I made the team and had a good year. That was 1940. The following season, I moved all the way up to Louisville in the American Association. The next year, I was a rookie with the Red Sox. The year after that, I joined the Navy.

Looking back, I was very fortunate in the service. Some fellows who came back from the war were never able to play again. Cecil Travis, for example, was an outstanding hitter for Washington but he got his feet frozen in the Battle of the Bulge. Phil Marchildon, a pitcher with the Philadelphia Athletics, was a gunner on a bomber which was shot down over Denmark. He also spent a year in a Nazi prisoner-of-war camp.

When I returned to the majors in '46, I was 25 years old but young enough that the skills came back right away. Everyone seemed happy to be back playing baseball and the Red Sox had one heck of a year. We got out of the blocks early and were virtually unbeatable at home. It looked like we were going to win for the next three or four years but, in '47, most of our pitching came up lame. That's baseball.

It's like the famous World Series play when Enos Slaughter scored all the way from first. That's what people remember or bring up when they talk about that particular Series. They remember me, too. You know, Pesky is a dumb so-and-so for holding the ball. Let's blame him. How come no one talks about the ninth inning? I guess people forget we had runners on first and third with one out but didn't score. They also forget about Harry Brecheen. He beat us not once, but three times!

We had some great hitting the years I was with the Red Sox. Few could do the things Ted Williams did. Ted would always tell me, "Do the things that you're capable of." One year, I had a chance to catch him in the batting race. I think Ted was hitting around .340 and he went into a slump. Some of the players thought I would overtake him because I sprayed the ball around to all fields. Just when it seemed I'd get close, Teddy would go off on one of his sprees.

The saddest day in my life as a ballplayer was the day the Red Sox traded me to Detroit. A lot of times, a ballplayer leaves the club and says his heart is out of it. Truthfully, I didn't feel that way. I was treated well in Boston. I didn't want to leave, but you go where they tell you because you have to make a living. Trades happen. I'd trade my brother if I could help my ballclub.

When I retired, I had no intentions of going into managing. I was a player-coach for Ralph Houk in Denver in '55. I played close to 90 games for him because the Yankees had Bobby Richardson, one of the best 19-year-old players I ever saw. Houk said to me, "Johnny, you can come back here if you want but why don't you try managing. I think you can do it." Tom Greenwade, the scout who signed Mickey Mantle, wanted me to go somewhere in Texas. I think it was Amarillo. It would have been a co-op team but with a youngster who was two or three years old, I wanted to go with an organization. I ended up working with the Tigers for five years, starting in Durham of the Carolina League and had some success.

In the minors, your main job is to develop youngsters. You're never going to be right all the time. Some can play hurt. Others can't. That's what you've got to try and understand. I'd rather lose a game than hurt a kid, whether it's a fielder, a hitter or a pitcher because his career is at stake.

I rejoined the Red Sox and managed two years in the Pacific Coast League. That Seattle team in 1961, for example, was one of the best clubs I've ever had. We had Arnold Earley, Bob Heffner, Hal Kolstad, Earl Wilson, Don Schwall, Bob Tillman, Lu Clinton, and Dick Radatz.

Radatz was a starter before he came to Seattle. He had a bad elbow so I stayed away from him because I had five or six starters. I was trying to balance off my ballclub so I called him to my office one day.

"Dick," I said, "did you ever think about relieving?"

"John," he said, "I don't want to do that. I don't know anything about it."

"Well, I'll teach you."

"If it means staying on the ballclub, I'll try it."

"I'll make a deal with you. If someone falters in the first five innings, I'll move you in."

"I can't ask for anything better than that."

The first week, I used Radatz four times. Each outing, he improved.

"Do you want to go back to starting?" I asked.

"Hell, no."

That's how the "Monster" was born. One time, I used Richard five days in a row and told him not to come to the ballpark. "Take your wife and children out to dinner," I said. "I'll pick up the tab."

The next day, guess who is at the ballpark.

"Well," he said, "the kids were making a lot of noise and I thought I'd come to the game just in case."

"Don't go near the bullpen."

Around the fifth inning, he's begging me to warm up.

"I feel fine," he said.

"Get your butt in the clubhouse."

An inning later, he comes out again, pleading to throw.

"John, I feel terrible," he said. "I haven't thrown 50 pitches this week."

Just to get him out of my hair, I sent him down to the bullpen.

We're in the 2-2 ballgame and it's now the eighth inning and Radatz begins to warm up. I'm watching him and he's watching me. We push a run home in the ninth to take the lead and in the bottom of the ninth, Portland threatens to score with two on and only one out. I look towards the bullpen. We had a sign that if you were warmed up and ready to go, the pitcher would touch his cap. I saw Radatz go to his cap and I then made the move.

Radatz comes in and he's firing bullets. He fanned the first guy on three pitches. The next batter popped up to end the game.

That's six straight days I used him.

"You're going to get me fired. When I send the reports to Boston and they see your name, 'Radatz in, Radatz in,' they're going to wonder what the hell I'm doing."

"John, it's just like getting a workout."

The way Radatz threw, you could use him four or five times week. If a ballgame was on the line, I never hesitated.

8

Eddie
Pellagrini

*T*he number "13" may suggest bad luck for some but not for Boston-born Eddie Pellagrini, who spent two of his eight big-league seasons with the Red Sox at Fenway Park.

"When I joined the Navy, I went overseas on ship number 13," says Eddie. "I got out of the service on the 13th. One year, I hit my 13th career homer on July 13th. One of my kids is my mother-in-law's 13th grandchild."

Pellagrini, who was born on March 13, 1918, finished with 13 career triples and 13 career stolen bases. In his 13th pro season in 1953, he wore No. 13 for the Pittsburgh Pirates. When he exited pro baseball and returned to his roots, Pellagrini wore No. 13 at Boston College until he retired from coaching in 1988.

"Looking over my career, 13 is my lucky number," says Eddie.

Primarily a reserve infielder, Pellagrini batted .226 in 563 games, including 96 with the Red Sox. He was a rookie on the '46 American League pennant winners when, on April 22, he homered to give Boston *a 5-4 victory over the Washington Senators in his first at-bat in the big leagues.*

After one more season in Boston, Pellagrini was shipped to the St. Louis Browns with five others and $310,000 for Vern Stephens and Jack Kramer. After two years with the Browns, Pellagrini was dealt to Cincinnati as part of a seven-player transaction and eventually finished his major league career with a two-year stint in Pittsburgh.

◆   ◆   ◆

All my life, I've been associated with teams that won. When I was in grammar school and high school, I played on teams that won league and city championships. I went away to play pro baseball and we won the pennant in 1938, 1939, 1940 and 1941. I joined the Navy and helped win the Second World War. I joined the Red Sox in 1946 and they won the American League pennant. Then the Red Sox sold me and it took them 21 years to win another one.

No doubt about it, that '46 club was one of the best teams that's ever played major league baseball. We had pitching, defense and hitting. Right from the start, we knew we were going to win. It's funny. You can tell when there's a feeling on a team. You could just sense it in the clubhouse. On the field, everything fell into place. Joe Cronin would put a guy in as a defensive replacement and he'd make a play to win a ballgame. After we won 15 straight, we knew.

I was a utilityman on that ballclub. I wound up in a slot where the shortstop ahead of me was a guy named Johnny Pesky who could hit .331 in his sleep. I always hit and played regularly in the minor leagues but I knew Pesky was going to play. What could I do, shoot him?

I believe I would have been in the big leagues in 1941 but then the war broke out. I was stationed at Great Lakes Naval Training Center and we had quite a team there. We won something like 65 games and lost only four. Mickey Cochrane was the manager and we had Hall of Famer Johnny Mize, Johnny Rigney of the White Sox, Johnny Lucadello who played with the Browns and Yankees and Barney McCosky of the Tigers. Rigney had some moves but the best one he ever made was marrying Dorothy Comiskey, the daughter of the White Sox owner.

After the service, I was never the same ballplayer. I knew it right away but I had a good spring and made the Red Sox, my hometown team. I was born in Boston and in those days, everyone was a free agent, but in my heart there was only one team I wanted to play for.

I had a couple of other offers but I signed with the Red Sox in 1938. My dad was from the old country and in the beginning he was against me playing sports. To him, baseball was a waste of time. Money was tough to make in those days. I'm sure others who grew up during the Great Depression will tell you the same thing. There were limited opportunities. My father wanted me to go to work and be a designer of clothes which isn't a bad job today. At the time, I couldn't draw a straight line.

My rookie year with the Red Sox I had only 71 at bats but I'll never forget my first time up. We're playing Washington and Mickey Harris and Sid Hudson were locked in a close game. We had home runs from Bobby Doerr and Rudy York and in the fifth inning, Hudson hit Pesky in the head with a pitch that bounced into the grandstand.

Cronin sent me in to run for Pesky and I had the jitters. You know, the hometown kid playing in Fenway Park. All I had been doing, up until that point, was sitting on the bench.

I come to bat in the seventh and Hudson got two quick strikes on me. The next pitch was real close but I didn't swing at it.

Al Evans, the catcher, said to me, "Bush, how can you take a pitch like that?"

"Good eye," I said.

When you're nervous, you say things or do things you don't normally do.

I guess my reaction activated my adrenal glands. I swung at Hudson's next pitch and the ball went over the fence. I ran around the bases so fast, they tell me my feet never touched the ground.

Now all that stuff about winning, there was no way I could help the St. Louis Browns. I don't think the good Lord, in all his glory, could have helped the Browns. It was a different kind of ballclub. This was a team which was used to losing year after year and did little to change things. You couldn't be an innovator because Zack Taylor, the manager, would get mad.

It was early in the season and I'll never forget this. I draw a two-out walk. I get down to first base and I start thinking, if I steal second, a hit can get me home and we can win the ballgame. I steal second base but that was as far as I advanced. We ended up losing the game so afterwards, Taylor called me in his office. I thought he was going to say something about the stolen base, like "Great play kid. A base hit and we would have won the game. Good hustle."

I was way off the mark.

"How come you stole second?" Zack asked.

"Well, there's two outs and if we get a base hit, we win the game."

"Did you get a sign?"

"No."

"From now on, you don't go anywhere unless you get a sign."

I'm thinking to myself, no wonder this team never wins.

In our final game that season, we beat the White Sox. I was going to drive from St. Louis to Boston with Tony Lupien who was born in Chelmsford and started his career with the Red Sox. At the time, Lupien was playing first base for Chicago. So after the game, the two of us talked about what time we were going to leave for home as the players left the field.

A few minutes passed before I got into the clubhouse and I couldn't believe what I saw. The guys were celebrating like the Browns had won the pennant. We only lost 94 games in 1948.

"We didn't lose as many games as last year," said Zack.

I'd like to believe it was the heat which may have disoriented the Browns but the weather didn't seem to bother the Cardinals. They always seemed to win.

One year, in the City Series Game, I reached first base. Stan "The Man" Musial was playing over there and we talked about the weather.

"Boy, it gets hot here," I said.

"Just wait," he said. "By the time summer comes, you'll be drained before you get to the ballpark."

I often wonder how high an average Musial would have hit if he played in the East. I got to figure at least 30 points more because he would have been stronger. In St. Louis, the nights are as hot as the days but the only difference is that the sun isn't out.

The year I spent in Philadelphia, I played for Eddie Sawyer and he was a great guy. The Phillies had won the pennant in 1950 and although they didn't have the pitching injuries we had in Boston, the players went through a similar situation. When you win, it seems, you celebrate all winter and believe what people said about how great you were. You come to camp a little cockier and you don't bear down enough. Before you know it, you're in third place and can't come back. We had a good team in Philadelphia but after I saw the Dodgers, I was really surprised that the Phillies won the year before.

People talk about the game in which Bobby Thomson hit the home run to beat the Dodgers as one of the greatest games in history. Well, we played Brooklyn in another one in 1951—the last game of the regular season. We were leading 8-5 but the Dodgers came back, tied the score and they beat us in the 14th on a home run by Jackie Robinson. I don't think anyone in the ballpark got up to go to the bathroom that day. No one.

Leo Durocher was the best manager I ever saw. Durocher, in my estimation, was a master of personnel. He played the game like it was a chess match. He'd move to the black to stop the red. I'll put in Billy Whoever. He knows how to bunt and it will get the runner over and then I'll get him out of there and put in this other guy to run because he can score from first base on a double. Leo had key guys for certain situations.

He used everyone and it worked. Every game was a messy box score because he played a lot of people.

Robin Roberts was one of the best pitchers I ever saw. I don't think Roberts could walk you if he wanted to. When he threw a baseball, you had better swing at it. If it was that far [Pellagrini uses his fingers to illustrate a space of about a half-inch] outside, and you took it, it was a strike.

I saw this happen plenty of times to Roberts. There would be two outs and someone would make an error. That's when you know you have a great pitcher because Roberts would go after the hitter. He went for the strikeout. Some pitchers feel sorry for themselves and wouldn't bear down, figuring they should be out of the inning and wouldn't care if they gave up a hit. Not Roberts. He never quit. He didn't want to give up that hit.

My next stop was Cincinnati and that's where I met Rogers Hornsby. I didn't know him too well but he must have been a great, great hitter. When I played for the Red Sox, this veteran player from California, whose name I forget now, was on the same team with Hornsby for eight seasons. He said that in his years with Hornsby, he never saw Rogers fooled on a pitch. Just think about that. The ordinary major league player, who is a good ballplayer in his own right, gets fooled quite frequently. Imagine playing eight years and not once getting fooled on a pitch!

In Pittsburgh, I played for Fred Haney, a manager who I always believed, if he ever had a competitive club, could win. Like Durocher, Haney could handle personnel. He didn't try to tell you how to play. He didn't overcoach or overmanage. You were a major league ballplayer so play. When you couldn't play, he'd put someone else in. That does a lot for a player. If you played for Haney and went 0-for-4, you knew you were going to play tomorrow. You could go hitless in a series but you'd still play because you're the better player. The proof was in the pudding when Haney won back-to-back championships and a World Series in Milwaukee.

I thought some day I'd go into managing because of the type of player I was. I used to ask a lot of questions, and try to gauge how people thought. I tried to remember what people said too.

One day in St. Louis, Dizzy Dean was broadcasting a game against Cleveland. Before the game, Dizzy was interviewing Satchel Paige in our dugout and I overheard the conversation.

"Satch, what happened last night?" Dizzy starts asking. "That guy hit a home run on you."

"He hit a 3-and-2 curveball and I don't like that," Paige said.

"What did you throw it for?"

43

"Well, my catcher put those two fingers down so I had to throw it."

"Would you throw the same pitch in the same situation?"

"I'll tell you one thing. I'll get them 3-and-2 again and they're going to have to beat me on my fastball."

I filed that bit of knowledge away for future reference. About a month or so later, we're playing in Cleveland and I'm batting against Paige who, regardless of how old he was back then, could still throw pretty good. I work the count to 3-and-2 and I know I got him. I'm thinking fastball and I'm geared for a good rip.

To this day, I'm still waiting for that fastball.

Satchel threw me a curveball and I just froze. There was nothing I could do but yell.

9

Joe
Dobson

When fans talk about successful Red Sox pitchers, Joe Dobson should be mentioned. The righthander spent eight of his 14 big-league years with Boston and produced a 106-72 record. Only once did he fail to post a breakeven ledger. A model of consistency, Dobson went 13-7 in 1946 as Boston reached the World Series. The following summer when several pitchers were scuttled with arm problems, Dobson had his best season—18-8 with a 2.95 earned run average.

Dobson, who established an American League record for pitchers by going 156 consecutive games before making his first error, started his career with Cleveland. He joined the Red Sox on December 12, 1940, in a six-player swap involving catcher Frank Pytlak and infielder Odell Hale for pitcher Jim Bagby, outfielder Gerald Walker and catcher Gene Desautels. Dobson remained a fixture in Boston until December 10, 1950, when he was traded to the Chicago White Sox, along with pitcher Dick Littlefield and outfielder Al Zarilla, for pitchers Ray Scarborough and Bill Wight.

Wearing different colored hosiery did not negate his effectiveness as Dobson went 26-21 over the next three seasons. He returned to Fenway in 1954 for a cameo two-game stint before calling it quits with a composite 137-103 record, a 3.62 ERA and a sharp .571 winning percentage.

While most remember Enos Slaughter's miracle dash which solved the '46 Series for St. Louis, it was Dobson who kept the vigil alive for the Red Sox. In Game 5, the righthander spaced four hits and went the distance— a 6-3 win—to give Boston a 3-2 lead in the best-of-seven set. In Game 7, Dobson also worked 2 2/3 innings of scoreless relief before the daring run by Slaughter.

◆　　　◆　　　◆

There are people who will tell you that I was a pretty good pitcher. When I read my scrapbook, it tells me I was a helluva pitcher. As I look at these clippings, I feel pretty good. . . the Red Sox and Fenway Park. When I was shipped out to Chicago for my last three years, that messed up the whole works.

I spent close to 20 years in baseball. It's my life. That's all I know.

I was born in Durant, Oklahoma, but our family left there when I was six years old. I was raised and educated in Coolidge, Arizona. In fact, I'm living in the same town right now. It's about 6,500 or 7,000 people. It's named after one of our presidents, Calvin Coolidge. Keep Cool with Cal.

Ever since I was big enough to have a ball in my hand, I wanted to play baseball. My brother was a pretty good player and we'd play catch every day. He'd throw that ball so hard, my hands would hurt.

Back in 1936, I played for a club out of Tucson. We were in a semi-pro tournament in Phoenix and had to play a doubleheader. I won the first game so I'm sitting in the stands waiting for us to win the second game. Anyway, we lost the game but a scout from the Cleveland Indians sent over for me. He wanted to know if I wanted to play professional ball. I would have paid him to sign me up.

The Indians trained in New Orleans and had some great pitchers. The first day, I walked out on the field, here comes Mel Harder. A real gentleman. He stopped and talked to me. That made everything. I was in a different world. Mel has been my favorite ever since.

At the time, this was 1939, Cleveland had about seven starters— people like Bob Feller, Al Milnar, Johnny Allen and Willis Hudlin. That spring, the weather was so cold, three or so of these guys couldn't pitch so I got a chance. I had a good spring too and made the ballclub. The Indians carried only two rookie pitchers, myself and Floyd Stromme. We both had a tough time finding work. Mostly, we'd sit in the bullpen, maybe warm up once in a while. We spent the bulk of our time picking splinters out of our rear ends. When the veterans started to come around, if Ossie Vitt needed an inning from someone, he'd send in one of his starters.

I started to get regular work by the latter part of 1940. Cleveland came into Fenway Park to play a doubleheader. Feller pitched the first game and won it in the eleventh or twelfth. I think it was a 2 to 1 game. I pitched the second game and shut Boston out. The funny part of this is I got Joe Cronin out pretty good. When I joined the Red Sox, I joked with Cronin that the only reason he traded for me was because he couldn't hit me.

I had spent two years in the minors and a couple of years in the big leagues, but truthfully, it wasn't enough time to learn the game properly. At the time, baseball didn't have pitching coaches. Teams may have had one or two who someone called a "pitching instructor" but my coach was the catcher who came over to Boston from Cleveland with me, Frankie Pytlak. Now, there was a smart catcher. He taught me how to pitch, change speeds and so forth.

Some people don't look at pitching as I do, but about sixty to seventy percent of the hitters are either high-ball hitters or low-ball hitters. The others are either in or out hitters. Against a .340 or .350 hitter, you do your best to get him out. If he hits one off of you, you hope no one else is on base. The key is to keep those .250 hitters off base.

In the '46 World Series, for example, our scouts had reports to pitch this guy this way and that guy another way. I went out there and the Cardinals started creaming me. So I told Roy Partee, "We might as well go back to our way of pitching." This was about the second or third inning of the fifth game. We forgot about the reports and I sailed right on through. No problem. I can't pitch like Boo Ferriss or Tex Hughson. I had to pitch my way. I was a curveball pitcher. To be successful, I had to change speeds.

An old-timer showed me how to throw a curve when I was a youngster. I threw it with my thumb up but he corrected me. You throw a curveball in a snapping motion. Snap your wrist in and down. Never extend your arm. The only way to learn to throw it is get a ball and throw it against a brick wall. Start throwing from ten or twenty feet. Keep snapping the ball. Get used to the motion. Once you do, keep backing up until you get to the right distance. Some think I'm full of baloney but my arm is still straight today. I've had bad tonsils and sore teeth but never a sore arm.

Ted Williams can tell you about my curveball. We had some fun in 1941, the year he hit .406. Early in the season I wasn't starting because Cronin had several pitchers he had to look at. I'm sitting back and waiting, but every day I'm throwing batting practice to Williams. Forty-five minutes at a crack. We'd have some ballgames out there. Imaginary ones but we still had our situations and battles. Ted loved to hit. Many times, he'd have blisters on his hands and they'd turn to calluses.

Bobby Doerr's in the Hall of Fame but he should have been in there the minute he got out of baseball. He was that good. What he could do with a glove! Before a game, we'd go over how we'd pitch the hitters. There were many a time I'd miss a spot. Now, a pitcher knows when a ball is hit hard. I'd turn around to see where the ball went. There's Doerr, picking it up and throwing the batter out.

Doerr won a couple of games for me against Feller at Fenway Park. Feller would dig a hole on the mound so deep, I'd have to fill it up and they'd start hollering from the dugout "Meow. Meow." I knew if I could stay even or close, like 1-0 or 2-1, we could beat him because Doerr could hit him.

Feller, though, had no match when it came to anyone with a curveball or fastball. What made Bob so effective, besides his fastball, was that he was a little bit wild. You never found too many toeholds up there at the plate. And his 3-and-2 curveballs were just nasty. The way his ball broke, you couldn't swing. You'd just freeze up there.

You can watch hitters from the dugout and learn how to pitch to them. See what they like and don't like. Jimmy Foxx was an exception. Could that man put a charge into a ball! So could Williams and Di-Maggio. I could name a bunch that could hit a ball a long way—Mantle, Berra. But the hardest to hit a ball was Foxx. He could hit a ball past an infielder well before he reached down for it. And the ball wasn't more than two feet out of the fielder's reach. One time, Foxx hit one over the flag in deep center. That ball went over everything. It's probably still floating up there with all that mess in the sky.

My career was interrupted by World War II. I didn't have to go overseas but I came close a couple of times. Patriotism didn't really occur to me because you had to go in. The Army was good for keeping you in shape. I was in the infantry. All we did was walk. I had no trouble keeping my weight at 190 pounds. I met some great people in the service and had a lot of fun. It was terrific. Just great guys. What I hated the most was the two years I lost because I was right in the middle of learning how to pitch. Maybe I could have won 200 games in the big leagues. I do know one thing. I was very fortunate. Others lost a heck of lot more than ballgames.

10

Sam
Mele

*S*am Mele, who had two terms of duty with the Boston Red Sox, never quite achieved prominence as a player during a 10-year career. But when he directed the Minnesota Twins to their first pennant in 1965, The Sporting News named him Manager of the Year.

Born Sabath Anthony Mele (the name S.A.M. is an acronym taken from his initials) on January 21, 1923, in Astoria, New York, Sam was a college basketball standout before signing a professional baseball contract with the Red Sox. After one season in the minors, Mele became a regular in right field as a rookie in 1947, batting a career-high .302 with 12 home runs and 73 runs batted in.

In his sophomore year, Mele took a reserve role and on June 13, 1949, he started his travels around the majors, first in a trade to Washington and later in deals involving the Chicago White Sox, Baltimore Orioles, Cincinnati Reds and finally with the Cleveland Indians in 1956. Overall, Mele batted .267 over 1,046 games with 80 home runs and 544 RBIs.

Mele's best season for production was 1951 with the Senators—leading the American League in doubles with 36 and netting a career-high 94 RBIs. His greatest moment as a player was June 10, 1952, when he tied two modern-day records for long hits (2) and RBIs (6) in one inning when he cleared the bases with a triple and slugged a three-run homer.

As for his managerial apprenticeship, Mele scouted and coached in Washington and when the franchise relocated to Minnesota, he took over the helm when Cookie Lavagetto was dismissed on June 23, 1961. Mele later met the same fate on June 9, 1967, despite a .548 winning percentage over seven seasons. He has since been a troubleshooter and scout for the Red Sox.

◆　　　◆　　　◆

Bill McCarthy was my baseball coach at New York University and on weekends he would take me to Fenway Park to work out with the Red Sox. I can't remember the year but what happened is something I'll never forget as long as I live.

I come out to hit early one morning with the Red Sox. I let one go by that looked off the plate and all I heard was this voice from behind the cage.

"Where was that pitch?"

"I took a ball," I said.

I never bothered to look at who had said it. I geared myself for the next pitch and I heard the voice again.

"You're right but the pitch was high enough to be a strike."

I took my last rip and I left the cage. The voice called me over and Ted Williams introduced himself.

Williams took batting practice each day like it was a game situation. A lot of ballplayers go up there just to see how many balls they can hit out of the ballpark. Not Ted. He'd start talking, saying something like "We're in the seventh game of the World Series. The count is 3-and-2, winning run on second." That's how he'd approach it.

Williams, for some reason, took a liking to me in spring training. He would always try to teach young fellows the game and on the bus he'd have me sit next to him. If we were going to, say, Tampa from Sarasota, the ride might be an hour and a half, maybe two hours. Ted would talk baseball and all I would do is listen. By the time I got off the bus, he convinced me I was one of the greatest hitters in the world.

I played in the same outfield with Williams and Dominic DiMaggio as a rookie in 1947. I wound up hitting .302 and I don't really know how I did it. I looked for all the help I could possibly get.

Wally Moses helped me a lot that year. He was playing right field for the Red Sox but was getting up there in age. Boston had tried Johnny Lazor, Leon Culberson and Tom McBride in the outfield and had traded George Metkovich to Cleveland. They were good ballplayers but I guess the Red Sox figured they wanted one player to play every day for them. It was ironic that Moses, of all people, was more or less helping me to take his job in spring training. He talked to me about the pitchers in the league, what their best pitch was, hitting the cutoff man and things like that.

DiMaggio was a great teacher, too. On our first road trip, we went to Philadelphia. I never had a roommate before and I didn't know what to expect. I just sat in the lobby and finally Dominic said, "All right, Mele. Get our bags." At first, I didn't know what he meant.

"You're rooming with me and since you're the rookie, take the bags up to the room. I want to show you who's the veteran on the ballclub."

Dominic taught me so much, I couldn't thank him enough. He was a great center fielder and he knew his way around Fenway Park. He'd give me a pointer or two about playing the caroms off the fence that juts out down the line in right field.

I played against Dominic's brother Joe in the service. I was in the Marine Corps and I was sent to boot training in San Diego. When that was over, we were shipped up to San Francisco and they put me on a carrier, the USS Long Island, which was kind of ironic because I was born on Long Island. On the way, I got sicker than a sonuvagun. I was just not a seafaring man. We had played some baseball games in San Francisco and when we finally pulled into Pearl Harbor, I was going up the ladder to the deck. As I neared topside, there's a big tough gunnery sergeant and he yelled out, "Does anybody here play baseball?"

All my friends knew that I did and said so.

"I want you to report to Lieutenant Reed tomorrow morning."

I played on the Marine baseball team for about seven months. We had a pitcher on the club, a lieutenant, who was in charge of the mess hall. He was one of the worst pitchers you ever saw in your life but we put him on the team so we could eat. Mornings after a game, we'd get steak and eggs. It got to a point that he was wondering when he was going to pitch because our manager hardly ever used him. In Hawaii, we played against the other military teams including the Army who had Joe DiMaggio, Joe Gordon, Mike McCormick and Walt Judnich.

When I was with the Red Sox, Dom introduced me to his famous brother. As you know, Joe is very quiet. Dom wasn't really that outspoken either but he said a little more than his brother. Matter of fact, Dom tells the story that when they passed each other on the field, it was:

"Hello, Dom."

"Hello, Joe."

It wasn't until they met later, maybe had dinner, that they said a little more to each other. They were two fabulous men.

From Boston, I moved to the Senators in a trade with Mickey Harris for Walt Masterson, a team I eventually moved into coaching with when I stopped playing. Washington had a young ballplayer I met in Indianapolis and later managed in Minnesota. Harmon Killebrew was recommended by a senator from Idaho and that fellow was probably one of the best scouts that's never been in baseball. Killebrew struck out a lot but when he hit a ball, he really hit it. He and I were together in the American Association and Harmon had an awful time making contact. Just terrible. He just worked and worked and that's what made him a better hitter.

Killebrew was a great team leader. Like DiMaggio, he didn't have to say much. The players simply looked up to him. The late Tom Dowd was the traveling secretary for the Red Sox and he asked me, when I was manager of the Twins, if I could get him one of Killebrew's bats. So one day, I asked Harmon if I could have one. He said, "You never asked for one in Indianapolis when I wasn't hitting the ball."

Killebrew's swing was geared for power. What helped him when I was in Minnesota is we had some players who could run and steal bases, people like Tony Oliva, Cesar Tovar, Zoilo Versalles and Ted Uhlaender. I told Harmon that I was going to have these players running a lot of times but I didn't want him hitting behind the runners. Killebrew was still striking out a good amount of times but I felt that, by sending men, he would likely concentrate more about making contact. He was able to raise his average about 25 points, into the .270s.

One time we were in a close game with Versalles on first base. I never had Killebrew bunt, never until this one particular day when I felt, I had to get Versalles in scoring position. With Killebrew, I had a runner in scoring position at the plate but for some reason, I gave Harmon the bunt sign. On the first pitch, you could tell he had never bunted in his life. I was wondering what I was making him bunt for so I took the bunt off. On the next pitch, the shortstop, figuring the bunt was still on, went over to cover second. Killebrew hit a line drive right where the shortstop would have been and Versalles ended up on third and eventually scored to win the ballgame. How dumb can a manager be, having a guy like Killebrew bunt? What made our Minnesota ballclub was getting Mudcat Grant from Cleveland, having a reliever like Al Worthington and a hitter like Tony Oliva. To this day, I don't understand why Oliva is not in the Hall of Fame.

When Oliva first joined the Twins, he didn't speak much English and I was fortunate to have Camilo Pascual as my interpreter. I had my coaches work with Oliva on fielding every day and he became one of the best outfielders in the league. Tony was a .315 lifetime hitter and could do everything. When he went to bat, we knew he was going to get a base hit and we'd have little wagers to guess where. Oliva could decide in a fraction of a second to take it to right field or go with a pitch to the opposite field.

I kid about why we lost to Los Angeles in the World Series in '65. It wasn't the Dodgers who beat us, it was the calendar. If the Jewish holiday season had two Yom Kippurs instead of one, Sandy Koufax wouldn't have pitched the last game.

The turning point in the seventh game was a play in the fifth inning by the late Junior Gilliam. Frank Quillici had doubled and I sent Rich Rollins up to bat for Jim Kaat and Koufax walked him. Versalles then hit a shot over the third base bag but Junior was able to backhand the ball and got a force play at third. Instead of it being a 2-1 ballgame and runners on first-and-third, we were done. Koufax didn't have his best curveball that day but he didn't need it. We were a good fastball-hitting team and Koufax beat us with fastballs.

After the game, I walked over to the Dodger clubhouse to congratulate Koufax. He was a pitcher I would pay just to watch warm up.

I shook his hand and Koufax said to me, "If I'm not mistaken, you hit a double off me in 1955."

"That's right," I said. "But do you recall the number of times you got me out?"

You have to figure, that if Koufax remembered that hit 10 years later, considering the way he pitched, he must have known every hitter inside-and-out. I played for Cincinnati in '55. In those days, Walter Alston hardly ever pitched Sandy because he was wild. This particular day, they brought him in and I doubled down the left field line.

I managed the Twins for close to seven years. Writers are always looking for something to write about and no matter what town I picked up a paper in, there was an article about Billy Martin looking over my shoulder and out to take my job. The simple truth is Martin helped me a great deal to be a good manager. He was a valuable coach and offered plenty of suggestions to me. There are times when it pays for a manager to be a good listener.

Because we won the pennant, I was automatically named to manage in the '66 All-Star Game. We're in Baltimore and I had to complete my roster, so naturally I select Mickey Mantle. This is a week or so before the game and I'm having breakfast with Martin. Billy gets a phone call and comes back and says Mickey's on the line and wants to talk to me. Mantle asked me if he could take the three days off because his legs were bothering him. Mantle played his whole career in pain. Because of that bad knee, he had tape from his ankles to his thighs.

"Mickey," I said, "if you want the three days off, it's okay with me."

Now, I have to name a replacement so I picked Tommie Agee of the Chicago White Sox. Agee was a heck of a ballplayer and was having a great season but there is no way you can replace a Mantle without some reaction somewhere.

Our next series happened to be in New York. We're staying at the Roosevelt Hotel and I received a phone call. The party on the other end of the line is using language I couldn't even begin to use the first letter of. I don't know why I'm listening to him but he ends the conversation with, "When you walk on the field, I'm going to shoot you and Tony Oliva."

If this banana shoots Oliva, he might as well shoot me. Where am I going to go without that guy?

I told my coaches about it. Calvin Griffith, our owner, was on the trip with us and he sent word to the Yankees. The incident was kept out of the newspapers but I remember looking in the stands that day and the Stadium was crawling with FBI men and special police, especially around our dugout.

I was nervous and I decided not to tell Oliva. That afternoon, I kept him on the bench, exactly where I wanted to be.

In the clubhouse, I asked Martin, "Billy, you always wanted to manage, right? Why don't you put on my uniform and bring the lineup to home plate?"

Billy caught on right away.

"Forget it," he said.

When it came time to bring out the lineup cards, I made sure I got right in the middle of the umpires. If any shooting was going to be done, the gunman would have to get all of us. Fortunately, nothing happened that day.

11

Walt
Dropo

*F*ew have broken into major league baseball in the same fashion *as Walt Dropo did in 1950. The "Moose" from Moosup, Con- necticut, was a logical choice for the American League's Rookie of the Year Award when you consider he was among the batting leaders at .322, was second in home runs with 34 and in slugging per- centage at .583, and shared the RBI crown with Vern Stephens at 144.*

While slugging numbers like these are difficult to maintain through- out one's tenure, Dropo was like a number of players who never came close to equalling a "career" season. But Dropo's power kept a number of teams seeking his services. In all, Dropo, a multi-sport standout in college at Connecticut, played for five teams during his 13 years in the majors—from 1949 to 1961—and batted .270 with 152 homers.

Dropo's time with the Red Sox consisted of 283 games and spanned four seasons. On June 3, 1952, Dropo was part of a major deal with Detroit that, he says, "did not help either team." However, within a month, Dropo tied a major-league record for most consecutive hits (12) to match a streak accomplished in 1938 by Mike Higgins of the Red Sox.

In 1954, as a member of the Chicago White Sox, Dropo took part in a brawl with the New York Yankees where "Enos Slaughter became the symbol of our battle because I ripped his shirt to shreds. All I wanted to be was a peacemaker."

◆   ◆   ◆

All my career I chased the Yankees. It seemed I was with teams that finished second or third. The Yankees won 10 pennants while I was in the big leagues and the only years they didn't win, Cleveland had to win 111 games and the go-go Chicago White Sox simply ran away from everybody.

Trying to make that Red Sox team was no easy task with people like Williams, Doerr, Pesky, DiMaggio and Stephens. They were all proven ballplayers. Boston had an established group of .300 hitters who had been around for eight, nine or 10 years. To tell you the truth, I never dreamed about having a season like I did in 1950. At the time, my goal was to play well enough and be lucky enough to make an impression. The pitchers challenged me with fastballs, insisting I couldn't hit the high, inside hard one. You hear people talk about not being able to hit a curveball but if you can't hit that one ball in the big leagues, you're as good as gone.

As a kid growing up, my idol was Ted Williams. I wanted to be just like him. They say life is full of strange circumstances. It's true. I wound up on the same team with that man and had a great year on his team.

I started in a little town of Moosup, Connecticut. In fact, my nickname "Moose" comes from a play on the name of my hometown. There are some who called me that, I'll bet, because I resembled a moose. After all, what else do you call a guy who stands 6-foot-5 and weighs 225 pounds?

My brothers, Myron and George, and I were bigger than most of the kids in our neighborhood and the teams we played on usually won. The three of us were always playing sports. There were no such things as Little League programs so my desire to play baseball just germinated from the sandlots to the town teams. During my time in the military service, I played with Ewell Blackwell and Harry Walker. The success I had against that degree of competition only made me feel confident that I had a chance to make it.

During my college days at UConn, I played three sports and excelled enough at football that the Chicago Bears drafted me. Sid Luckman and George Halas had a heck of a team back in those days but they didn't have money to pay the players. Television was in its infancy and a great star like Bulldog Turner, a top-flight lineman, was making $5,000 a year. Halas was going after players from small schools, hard and rugged guys who played at little, out of the way places like Hardin-Simmons rather than say Alabama or Georgia. Halas thought I could really develop into quite a football player, but deep down I wanted to play baseball.

Money is usually the turning point in any decision and that was the major reason why I signed with the Red Sox. Halas tried to work a deal with Mr. Wrigley where I would play baseball in the summer with the Cubs and football in the fall with the Bears but Mr. Yawkey was a very, very generous man when it came to money. I received a good bonus to sign, $15,000. The Red Sox also were going to pay me $600 a month. To me, that was all the money in the world.

My first stop was in the Eastern League. Eddie Popowski was the manager and the day I get to Scranton, I'm handed a first baseman's mitt. In my first game against Wilkes-Barre, Mike Garcia struck me out four straight times.

"Eddie, I get the feeling I'm in the wrong league," I told Popowski. "I can't hit this pitching."

All "Pop" told me was to come to the ballpark at 10 a.m. every day. "We'll make you into a player," he said.

I can remember my hands being so callused. Every day, without fail, I was taking extra hitting and fielding. In a matter of time, I finally caught up with the league. I hit 12 homers and batted .297. The Eastern League was my indoctrination. It took a while to grasp what the game was all about. There is a big difference from college ball to a league where guys are changing speeds and have control of two or three pitches. No one in the league was a proven player but as long as I was growing with the others, improving and all, I felt I was getting an idea of what to do. The next year in Birmingham, I knocked the hell out of the Southern Association, batting .359. Our team won the Dixie Series. I knew I was knocking at the door.

In 1949, I was up for a few games with Boston and the season I'm remembered for, 1950, I didn't even begin the year in Boston. I started with Louisville and we had played, maybe a dozen games. We're in Indianapolis for a series and I get a call from Mike Ryba to go to breakfast. I had no idea what he was going to tell me. I've missed a few curfews in my time but that particular night, I had checked in early.

"Go to the ballpark and get packed," Ryba said.

I asked where I was going.

"Boston. Goodman broke his ankle and they need a first baseman."

I finish my breakfast, head to the ballpark to get my equipment and eventually catch a plane to Logan Airport. I arrive about 11 p.m. I haven't been on the ground five minutes and Clif Keane, a writer the players nicknamed the "Poison Pen," is telling me, "Dropo, Goodman's ankle isn't hurt that badly. You'll be here only a couple of weeks. You'll be back with Louisville."

"The hell with Louisville," I told him. "I'm not going back to Triple A. I'm here to help this ballclub. You can print it. I'm not leaving."

The next day, I'm in a headline which read: **Dropo will not report back to Louisville.** I'm not in the big leagues 24 hours and I've already put myself on the spot. I'm opening up against Cleveland who only has a pitching staff of Feller, Wynn, Lemon and my good friend Garcia. Here I am, telling everybody, that I'm not going to go back to the minors when I haven't even made the team.

I was joining a team loaded with offense. Where do you find at-bats with guys like Williams, Doerr, Pesky, DiMaggio, Zarilla and Stephens? Fortunately, I got off to a good start, hit the ball real good. The newspaper guys wondered when I was going to cool off a bit but I kept saying that my goal was to help the team. Birdie Tebbetts told me "three games doesn't make a season" so I had the motivation to keep working and show the others I possessed the skills to stay with the big club.

Boston was a unique situation for me. The Monster just sits out there. Psychologically, you know the Wall is there. In some ways, I think, it hurt me because I became a dead pull hitter. That Wall didn't only catch me. Plenty of others got caught in that trap, too.

The Red Sox put up some numbers in 1950. We hit .302 as a team and our defense was among the best in the league but we fell short by a few games to the Yankees. They had plenty of pitching with Lopat, Raschi, Reynolds, Byrnes, Ford and Page coming out of the bullpen. Pitching will dominate good hitting and we just didn't have enough behind Parnell and Kinder. We also went a stretch without Williams. Ted fractured an elbow in the All-Star Game running into the fence trying to catch Kiner's fly ball or at least that's what everyone thought. He was still playing in the eighth inning. Ted was due to hit against Jansen and Stengel asked him if he was okay.

"Casey. Give me a bat. I'll get a hit," is what Williams said.

That's exactly what Williams did. After the hit, Casey replaced him with a pinch-runner. The next day, the doctors operated on Teddy Ballgame.

I have a lot of emotions about the players of my time. Williams is the Picasso. . .a Michelangelo with the bat. The Messiah. Call him anything you want. No one could handle a bat like he could. When I came into the league, I was as big as Ted, as strong as he was and maybe smarter since I went to college. To myself, I felt I could do what he did. But the only thing you can't measure accurately is the split-second to swing the bat and get square wood on the ball. That is something Williams did better than anyone else I saw play. Two other great talents were Frank Robinson and Brooks Robinson. I was with Cincinnati when Frank won the Rookie of the Year Award and I watched Brooks in Baltimore make plays that no one else with a glove could make. But no one could swing a bat like Williams.

I had the good fortune to play on teams with some great players, observing like a hawk and trying to pick up a thing or two. One game against the Yankees, Reynolds, who could throw, got Williams. As Ted walked back to the dugout, he said to me, "Busher, the Chief's quick today." You knew that the pitcher had more than just speed. You had to be ready.

Or Kaline. The Tigers signed this 18-year-old kid out of high school in Baltimore. Detroit gave this slim guy $50,000. Just looking at him, I'd guess I was worth $100,000. Kaline would be working out with us and guys like Pat Mullin, Ray Boone, Harvey Kuenn and myself, would ask one another "What does Detroit see in this kid?" About a month later, we had our answer and Kaline left us in the dust.

12

Lou
Boudreau

*O*n November 25, 1941, Lou Boudreau, then 24 years old and emerging as a quality shortstop, became the youngest manager in American League history when he was given the reins by the Cleveland Indians.

Whether he was making sparkling plays in the field with the glove, slamming clutch hits or designing a strategy to rattle Ted Williams, Boudreau produced results. He led the league in fielding seven of his first eight seasons and was a respected performer over his 15 seasons in the majors. He is one of a handful of players—the only one in the AL—to collect five extra-base hits in one game, ripping four doubles and a home run on May 14, 1946. In 1970, he joined the greats in Cooperstown.

Born July 17, 1917, in Harvey, Illinois, Boudreau won the batting crown in 1944 with a .327 average and had three other .300 seasons. He is best remembered for 1948, his Most Valuable Player season, when he batted .355 with 18 home runs, 116 runs scored, and 106 runs batted in—all career highs. One of his best days was in a playoff game against the

Red Sox at Fenway Park—two homers and four hits—which sparked an 8-3 win on October 4 and a date with the Boston Braves in the World Series.

"I'll never forget that Monday afternoon," says Boudreau. "It was quite a thrill. We had a great celebration party that night, too. I had a scheduled workout the next day at Braves Field but it wasn't that well attended. Most of my guys were trying to sober up. I was concerned but not as much as I was a week or so later waiting for Bob Kennedy to catch that fly ball to clinch the Series." Against the Braves, Boudreau batted .273 with four doubles to help the Tribe capture its first championship since 1920.

When ownership changed in Cleveland, Boudreau was released after the 1950 season. He signed with the Red Sox and batted .267 in 82 games as a reserve infielder. In 1952, he succeeded Steve O'Neill as manager and stayed at the helm for three seasons, a period when the Red Sox were in transition. His best year was 1953 when the Sox finished fourth at 84-69.

Once leaving the Bosox, Boudreau went on to manage the Kansas City Athletics for three seasons and later spent a year as the skipper of the Chicago Cubs. He has also worked in broadcasting.

◆　　　◆　　　◆

Boston was, and still is, a wonderful sports town. The fans are tremendous and really support the Red Sox. I'll tell you one thing—everyone hates to lose but the Red Sox fans hate it a little bit more. They know what winning means and they want to win. Over the years, they have had good baseball teams, and also the best player I ever saw.

When I did join the Red Sox, I was frightened a bit, figuring that Ted Williams would have something to say about my years in Cleveland. I'm credited with that infield shift used against Ted. Because of what the other players had told me, I knew Ted was angry about it. Whenever Williams made an out against that shift, I'm told, he would knock out the lights in the tunnel leading to the clubhouse. We kept charts in those days and we were something like 32 percent better when we put four fielders on the right side of the diamond. I often wondered what I would have done if Ted had ever bunted the first time we tried it!

I'm not taking anything away from Stan Musial or the others but when it came to hitting, Williams, to me, was the best. Seeing Ted play and then going over to manage him with the Red Sox and watching what he could do every day, I'm prejudiced towards Williams. He had a little restaurant up at the Cape and he'd drive there, about an hour after a ballgame. On several occasions, he invited me out to dinner with him but he never once mentioned the shift to me. We'd settle down in a corner and enjoy a good eat.

My one regret in baseball was that I couldn't go or have a close association with teammates who were my age because I was the manager and couldn't show favoritism. Because I was so young when I was managing, I would only be with the sportswriters and coaches, who were older.

I wound up as manager of the Indians because of a man named Joseph Martin. Roger Peckinpaugh managed the club in 1941 and after the season, ownership pushed him up to vice-president so the job of manager was vacant. I wrote a letter to Alva Bradley, the club president, about the position. I listed my credentials and the reasons why I should be not only considered for the job but hired. I guess it was a rather bold try on my part. Before I signed with Cleveland, I captained the basketball team at the University of Illinois so I figured I could do the job.

I was one of several people interviewed. The ownership of the club took a vote and I lost by an 11-1 margin. The only man who voted for me was Mr. Martin. He was about 82 years old. I guess he gave a great speech to the other partners. The Indians had something like six managers in eight seasons and Mr. Martin felt that a young guy could do as good a job as the others. He also believed that if I was hired, the team should hire veteran coaches to help me. That sold the partnership and that's how I became the youngest manager in league history.

I was a bit skeptical of how it would work. Cleveland had a veteran team and I wasn't sure how the older guys would respond. What was even more of a challenge was that four of the older guys had applied for the manager's job! But things have a way of working out for the best. That group was as helpful as any group of men you'll find.

When Bill Veeck bought the ballclub, one of the best moves he recommended to me was to name Bill McKechnie as one of our coaches. McKechnie managed in Cincinnati for a number of years and I have to credit him for making Bob Lemon into a 20-game winner. With McKechnie around, it was like two 100-pound sacks of cement were lifted off of my shoulders. Veeck had a way of promoting sports like no one else. We always had giveaway days and indirectly, one of the biggest, I guess, was the situation he found himself in when word leaked out during the 1947 World Series that I was going to be traded to the St. Louis Browns. Veeck was plotting a trade of myself, and outfielders George Metkovich and Dick Kokos, to the Browns for shortstop Vern Stephens, pitchers Jack Kramer and Ellis Kinder and outfielder Paul Lehner. The result was a public outcry. The newspapers conducted a poll, with a ballot on the front page where fans could vote as to who they wanted to manage the Indians in 1948. There was something like 100,000 responses and 90 percent of the voters wanted me to remain. You never know how many friends you have until a situation arises.

During the war years, we didn't have a strong team but the seeds of our championship club began when Veeck took over. What solidified our club was getting an every day player from the Yankees named Joe Gordon for Allie Reynolds. Gordon made me as a fielder. I wasn't the fastest around but Gordon made up for my shortcomings. He, Ray Mack and Bobby Doerr were the best second basemen I ever played alongside.

In recent years, the importance of defense is finally getting its due. They are voting shortstops into the Hall of Fame like Pee Wee Reese and Luis Aparicio. Phil Rizzuto and Marty Marion should be there, too.

I'll tell you what made the Yankees a great team. You can talk all you want about pitching, and in Cleveland, we had as good a group as New York, but check the Yankee defense and start with Rizzuto at short. In the outfield, DiMaggio was flanked by Henrich and Bauer. Joe wasn't the flashy, Willie Mays type but he found a way to get to the ball. Come the seventh, eighth or ninth inning, Joe would give that little extra. You were not going to get an extra base on him.

People, for some reason, tend to talk about things that others don't accomplish. Everyone knows Bob Feller never won a Series game but that doesn't detract from what that man did. Feller threw no-hitters, one-hitters, and struck out everyone who has ever played at least twice. He was truly a great, great pitcher.

I started Feller in the Series opener. He pitched a two-hitter and got beat 1-0. It was a nothing-nothing game that was decided by a pickoff play and a single on the next pitch to Tommy Holmes. In Game 4, Bob Elliott hit two home runs off Feller but our whole pitching staff got shellacked that day.

But getting back to that pickoff play, I knew on October 6, 1948, that we had Phil Masi dead at second base but it wasn't until recently that Masi finally changed his story. I would be at banquets with him over the years and he always maintained that umpire Bill Stewart made the right call. Phil never admitted that he was out until Stewart passed away. I guess he felt it was okay to finally admit the truth.

13

Johnny Lipon

*T*here will always be organization men in baseball, former players whose primary task is developing talent for the major leagues. For a short time in 1971, Johnny Lipon wrote lineups for the Cleveland Indians. For the most part, Lipon has made a career out of managing future pros, lately in the South Atlantic League.

Born in Martin's Ferry, Ohio, on November 10, 1922, Lipon grew up in Michigan and eventually signed a baseball contract with the Detroit Tigers. An infielder, Lipon spent nine years in the majors, also playing for the Boston Red Sox, St. Louis Browns and Cincinnati Reds. He had a lifetime .259 batting average but is best remembered for his glovework. In 1950, Lipon led American League shortstops in several fielding categories and on May 20, he tied a league record by participating in five double plays in one game.

Lipon's stay in Boston consisted of 139 games, divided over two seasons, 1952 and 1953. He arrived in a controversial multi-player swap with Detroit and was later sold to the Browns. Upon retiring, Lipon *started his managerial career, a trek that has taken him throughout baseball cities of North America since 1959. Today, Lipon manages Detroit's farm club in the Florida State League at Lakeland.*

◆   ◆   ◆

I'll never forget my first at bat in the big leagues. I faced Eddie Smith of the Chicago White Sox. His first pitch was about a foot over my head and Bill McKinley called it a strike.

Umpires, you know, like to see how a rookie will react but I never said a word. I was so nervous, I didn't even turn around. On the next pitch, I hit one off the fists and was fortunate to single to center field.

My next time up, McKinley was dusting off the plate and turned to me. "Hey, kid," he said, "how come you didn't say anything to me in the first inning? That pitch was a little high."

I told him I didn't know what the strike zone was in the American League.

Well, McKinley had a good laugh and from that time on, I had a good rapport with the umpires.

I have called Detroit home since my family moved there when I was five years old. Dad was a coal miner and I was born in a company house of a mining village. There were eight of us in the family but it wasn't big by standards back then. I recall a Lithuanian couple, two doors down, who had 18 kids.

Dad wanted us to get an education and go to college, but I wanted to play baseball. Charlie Gehringer was my boyhood idol. In high school, I worked out with the Tigers and Pinky Higgins let me use his glove. The Tigers wouldn't let me hit but Wish Egan, the man who eventually signed me, let me swing one day. He gave me the heaviest bat he could find. It was broken too. The first three pitches, I went down on my rear.

When you first start playing professional baseball, you don't know if you belong. I got off to a slow start in Muskegon of the Michigan State League but after a month and a half, everything fell into place. I started to hit homers and even the check swings fell in for hits. I led the league in several categories including errors. I think Gene Woodling edged me for the batting title by a half of a point.

My next stop was in the Texas League. Beaumont was the hottest place on earth but it worked in our favor. It was like anything else if you go into it with a positive attitude. Steve O'Neill, our manager, would say, "The heat don't bother us. When the other team comes in, we'll laugh at them. Their pitchers will run out of gas." It was true. Opposing pitchers had trouble lasting four or five innings. They'd strike out two or three of us early. Come the sixth inning, they wouldn't be in there. I batted over .300 that season but hit only three homers. They used a dead ball and you could not hit it for any distance. That's where the "Texas League" single originated. I think eleven home runs led the league.

I joined the Navy to fight in a war our generation thought would end all wars. Patriotism was the big thing. Everyone hated Hitler after the atrocities. No one liked Japan because of the Pearl Harbor thing so we were pretty much gung-ho. It wasn't like the Vietnam conflict. I can understand why the kids didn't favor it. World War II was a popular war. You went in the service because your friends went in.

I had only played a few games in the major leagues but your reputation goes wherever you go. Mickey Cochrane wanted me to play baseball for him at Great Lakes but I wanted to go fight. I went to mechanic's school at Millington Naval Air Base with Hal Schumacher. I played a couple of games there before I left for gunnery school in Jacksonville, Florida.

I ended up as a flight engineer aboard the V-H 2 rescue squadron in the South Pacific. We were based on Guam and the Mariana Islands. That's where I spent most of my time. We did, however, go into Iwo Jima and help evacuate some of the Marines and the Army. I was assigned to a P.B.M., an amphibious aircraft. A Patrol Bomber Mariner. Our mission was to circle the area where our fighter planes would be coming back from bombing raids and pick up anyone in trouble. If the ocean wasn't too rough, we'd land on the water but we'd mostly drop life preservers until a ship could come to complete the rescue.

During the 40 months I was in the service, I developed bursitis. I did not play much in 1946 when I returned to the Tigers. I couldn't throw a ball across a room much less across a baseball diamond. It was a wasted year, but I never complained about it. A lot of guys who went to war never came back or were worse off than me. An infielder named Joe Wessing was the best second baseman I ever played with. We were together at Beaumont and he was quick on the double play. Sort of like Bill Mazeroski. Joe could never play after the War. He was in the infantry and he walked for those three years with that heavy pack on his back. Because of the walking, he developed a different set of muscles and had all types of hamstring problems.

I took all kinds of treatment but I was a frustrated young man. It looked like my future was clouded. Not only that, I also lost my power. From not playing for three years, I could not hit a ball to the left field fence at Briggs Stadium. Four years before, I could hit a ball into the upper deck. I lost timing and never did regain it. The Tigers sent me to Dallas in 1947 and my arm was killing me. I kept throwing and throwing and finally, it got better but I never had the strength I used to have.

I finally started for the Tigers in 1948 and had a good year. I hit .290, and the guy I respected the most on that club was Freddie Hutchinson.

He was tough as a grizzly and he knew how to pitch. He lost his velocity and became a breaking ball pitcher. Hutch had a good pickoff move too. That year, we nailed 10 or 12 guys at second base.

The biggest game of the season was our last. It was Bob Feller against Hal Newhouser. If the Indians won, they would clinch the pennant. There were 70,000 people in Municipal Stadium and I never saw more disappointed fans. There was not a peep in the ballpark. That forced a playoff game in Boston and Lou Boudreau had that big game. He was fine hitter.

Cleveland paid us back in 1950. We won 95 games that year and should have won the pennant. We had a four-game lead with two weeks to play and our hitting quit. We lost two of three in Philadelphia, split in Washington and got whipped by the Indians.

Ted Williams was the best hitter I ever saw but the years I played in Boston, Ted spent most of the time in Korea. He seemed to hit everything on the fat part of the bat. Even if he popped up, it was a mile high. A ground ball was a shot. You didn't see many pitchers fool him, whether they were left-handed or right-handed. Normally, a lefty doesn't do that well against left-handed pitching but Ted murdered them. I know. He murdered Newhouser. Hal couldn't get him out.

I came to the Red Sox as part of a controversial trade in 1952. Both teams were making changes and the deal really upset the fans. You trade favorites and no one likes it in either city. I know Detroit did not want to lose George Kell, Hoot Evers and Dizzy Trout any more than Boston wanted to lose Johnny Pesky, Walt Dropo, Fred Hatfield, Don Lenhardt and Bill Wight.

I was traded again in 1953 and spent the last two weeks of the season with Satchel Paige and the St. Louis Browns. In high school, I hit against Satchel when he pitched against a semi-pro team I played for in Detroit. He pitched seven innings that day and struck out 18 of us. I don't know how old he was when he pitched for the Browns, but he still could throw hard. The ball was like a little ping-pong ball coming to the plate.

I'll tell you one thing, the blacks added talent and speed to the game. Most teams tried to copy the Yankees. All power. One inning, they'd score six runs and beat you. It was tough to argue with success. There was no reason to steal bases. But here comes Jackie Robinson making things happen for the Dodgers. Many teams went to the running game.

I admire the blacks. Color should not make a difference. Back then, there was bigotry and no understanding. Some restaurants would not feed them. It was not a good situation. Blacks resented it and you can't blame them. I'm from Polish descent. I remember stories too, so I can understand their point. My dad was an immigrant. Here I am, a first generation American and I'm a dumb Polack. If you got away from your area, you'd have to fight your way through some times. Life was tough then. Heck, it's tough today. The country has made great strides during my lifetime but the world is changing so quickly you hope this generation can cope. Just look what the computer has done.

My last at bat in the big leagues was in 1954 for Cincinnati. I hit a fly ball to left field. That was my only time up in the National League. I had some back trouble and had slowed down noticeably. My arm was still hurting but I had a chance to play for a team in Cuba. Havana had a Triple A club in the International League. Havana was a gambling and entertainment city just like Las Vegas. Horse racing, dog racing. They also had outstanding baseball fans who liked to bet. They wagered on every pitch, if it was going to be a ball or a strike. The people helped us win and danced when we had those late inning rallies.

My first managing job was in the Alabama-Florida League in 1959. I have a funny story about that season in Selma. We had a second baseman, a scrappy kid, on our club. He did not have a hit in 25 trips or so and I benched him. We're in a game one night, playing extra innings. I had to pinch-hit for a pitcher who couldn't hit at all, so I sent this kid up to bat. Now there were about 450 fans at the ballpark and they start booing. I told this kid not to worry about the noise.

"Get a hit and they'll quiet down," I said.

"Skip," he said. "They're not booing me. They're booing you."

I managed Sam McDowell in the Pacific Coast League in 1964. When I was coaching in Cleveland in 1968, I saw him strike out 40 men over a three-game stretch. He really had a fantastic arm. People expected a lot from Sam but he didn't have the control a pitcher who consistently wins 20 games needs. He'd always have one bad inning where he'd walk two or three. I hate to hear people say Sam wasted a career even though he had a few drinking problems. He had some pretty good pitchers going against him too. He'd face the Denny McLains and others having big years. I think he had better stuff but he pitched himself out of too many games. Sam couldn't control his wildness. If he ever did, he would have been another Koufax.

When Alvin Dark was fired, I took over the Cleveland job for the tail end of '71. I was told to play the kids so we played John Lowenstein at second and Kurt Bevacqua at third. We pitched guys like Ed Farmer and used rookies like Ted Ford and Frank Baker in the outfield to see what they could do. The Indians did not offer me the job for 1972 so I never really got a chance to manage in Cleveland. But looking back on it, it was probably the best thing that ever happened. I've had an opportunity to watch many young players become fine managers, people like Sparky Anderson and Chuck Tanner who both played for me in Toronto in 1961.

Lou Piniella was with me in Portland in 1967. God, that guy would drive you crazy. Himself too. That year, we had a punching bag set up in the clubhouse for him. One time he hit the bag so hard, it came back and smacked him right in the face.

I believe most big league managers have more problems than I'll ever have. Strategy-wise, I'm as good as anyone who has ever lived except for Casey Stengel or the other fabulous names. Baseball is the same game. Nine men are out there, and to win, you have to get 27 outs.

14

Frank
Malzone

*I*n a vote by Red Sox fans in 1969 to help baseball celebrate its 100th
birthday, Frank Malzone earned a flood of support from the Fenway
faithful for a position on Boston's all-time team. It was quite a tribute
for Malzone, a durable and productive performer, the mainstay at
third base from 1957 to 1965.

Born in New York on February 28, 1930, Malzone signed with the Red
Sox in 1948 after graduating from high school to launch his long associa-
tion with the ballclub. After several years in the minors, his debut at
Fenway was a signal of good things to come—six hits in 10 at bats against
Baltimore on September 20, 1955.

Until his departure in 1966 to the California Angels for one season,
Malzone played 150 or so games annually for the Bosox, drove in between
80 and 90 runs and was good for 15 to 20 home runs. A perennial All-
Star selection, Malzone had a career .274 batting average and 133 lifetime homers.

With the glove, Malzone had a career .950 fielding percentage while *playing over 1,400 games at the hot corner. He shares an American League record for leading the circuit in double plays (five times). He was also named to three Gold Glove Fielding Teams by* The Sporting News.

◆   ◆   ◆

You know I always chuckle when I hear someone say, "Well, you can put anybody at third base." What a fallacy that is. Over the years, people have found out that third base is one of the toughest positions to play for one simple reason. You don't see the pitch like the middle infielders. The shortstop and second baseman can lean a bit or play the pitch because they have the play in front of them. You don't have that luxury over at third.

Once you get to know the hitters in the league, third base can become easier to play. Each team has one or two guys who like to bunt. That keeps you on your toes but bunting is a lost art in today's game. The hitters come in now and try to hit the ball on a straight line drive.

Everyone is so number conscious today. We were too, but not as much as today. In a way, you can't blame the players. The agents put numbers in front of them. The agent determines how much money you're going to ask for. That's what the game is all about. I'm not knocking the modern-day player because many have the ability to play but some are still learning how to play the game. Years ago, if you made two mental mistakes in a row, they'd send you back to Triple A. The attitude was "Go back and learn how to play."

Growing up in the Bronx, about the only thing I knew about professional baseball was that the Yankees, Giants and Dodgers played in New York. As a kid, you know, you say well heck, I can't play with these guys. If I had given it more thought, I probably would have wanted to be a big-league ballplayer.

Cy Phillips was a bird dog for the Red Sox and worked out of New York. At the time, he owned a sporting goods store and he had seen me play in high school and for a couple of semi-pro teams.

One day he asked if I'd be interested in professional baseball. At the time, I went to Samuel Gompers, a vocational school, and was planning to be an electrician. In fact, I was already accepted in that position by Con Edison. Had the interview and everything. When the baseball opportunity came along, I knew one thing. If things didn't work, I could always go back to Con Ed.

I spent several years in the minors but also had a hitch in Korea. I was in the Army if you want to call it that. I went to my interview for boot camp in Camp Kilmer, New Jersey. I remember the sergeant asking me if I wanted to go to Hawaii for basic training. "No," I said. "I'd just as soon not. You know, just stay around here." Anyway, I ended up on a boat going to Hawaii. I actually played for the Army baseball team. We didn't have to go into formation too much because the colonel liked baseball. Our base had a pretty good team. Don Larsen was one of our pitchers.

After the service, I spent two years in Louisville. At the time, Boston was going through changes. George Kell was finishing up his career and the Red Sox had just spent some bonus money on guys like Bill Consolo and Ted Lepcio and wanted to find out about them.

I was sitting in the background, waiting for a chance. I wasn't a big guy but nobody ever classified me as being small. I was almost five-ten, but because I put numbers on the board, I didn't hit like a small guy. In 1955, I played practically every day in spring training for whatever team the Red Sox assigned me to. That season at Louisville, I hit .310 and drove in 88 runs. If I was in their plans, I think 1956 was the year they were counting on for me to be their third baseman.

During the winter, my family suffered a personal tragedy. My wife and I lost our first child. She was just fourteen months. When spring training opened, I wasn't worth nothing. It really affected me. You never get over it but I knew this misfortune was bothering my wife more. The two of us never got straightened out until we met a priest who understood our situation. He sat us down and talked. He gave us the right information. Eventually, everything worked out. I got back on track and had a good year in the Coast League.

I don't know what took place the next year in spring training, but I thought I wasn't going to make the club. I rode the bench for the first couple of weeks and I figured I wasn't going to get a chance. Oddly enough, the Red Sox went out to San Francisco to play a series of exhibitions. One of the players came to me and said, "Guess who's playing today?" I was in the lineup for that game and every other game that spring. I wound up on the parent club and played the whole season.

I had a pretty productive year for a rookie. Everything took place that year but the thing I treasure the most about 1957 is my first Gold Glove. At the time, they gave one fielding award and I beat all the National Leaguers, too. I kid Brooks Robinson that I have one glove he's never going to get.

Brooks, Clete Boyer and I competed against each other, year in and year out. Brooks is Brooks and Clete was also talented. He could field but what helped him was the recognition that goes by being on a pennant winner. Mention Frank Malzone to people, the only ones who really know me are the Boston or New England people because they saw me play regularly. Around the country, people remember you if you played in the World Series. Being on a winner makes all the difference.

◆ FENWAY VOICES

Take players today. Carlton Fisk was well-known when he played in Boston. People remember him waving his arms, helping that home run he hit stay fair. Now he's with the White Sox. It's a little different. Players like Fisk, Lynn and some of the others who left the Red Sox were fortunate they played on winners when they were here.

15

Mickey Vernon

*S*lick-fielding Mickey Vernon is one of a handful of major leaguers
to play in four different decades. In the late 1950s, the lanky first
baseman played 221 games for the Boston Red Sox.

Vernon, who batted .286 lifetime and socked 172 home runs,
won the American League batting crown in 1946 (.353) and in 1953 (.337)
but is remembered more for his glovework. During his career, Vernon
established several fielding records, including the modern day major
league record for most career games played by a first baseman (2,237) and
the major league mark for most double plays (2,044). In addition, Vernon
holds several American League fielding marks, including most putouts
(19,754), most assists (1,444) and most chances (21,198).

Born April 22, 1918, in Marcus Hooks, Pennsylvania, Vernon began
his baseball career in the St. Louis Browns chain in 1937 but was released. Vernon's long association with the Washington Senators started the
following year. Except for a military hitch and a 181-game stint with the
Cleveland Indians in 1949 and 1950, Vernon was the regular first
baseman for the Nats from 1941 to 1955.

◆ FENWAY VOICES

On November 8, 1955, Vernon joined the Red Sox along with pitchers Bob Porterfield and Johnny Schmitz and outfielder Tommy Umphlett in exchange for pitchers Dick Brodowski, Tex Clevenger and Al Curtis and outfielders Karl Olson and Neil Chrisley. In his first crack at Fenway, Vernon batted .310 with 15 homers and 85 runs batted in. After another summer with the Bosox, Vernon finished his playing career with one-year stops in Cleveland, Milwaukee and Pittsburgh. Upon retirement, he managed the expansion Senators from 1961 to 1963.

Vernon has remained in baseball in several capacities, as a coach in the big leagues and as a minor league manager and instructor. Today, he is a special scout for the New York Yankees.

◆　　　◆　　　◆

I wish I would have joined the Red Sox 10 years earlier because everything about the Boston scene was great. Ted Williams and I were good friends. I'm not a fisherman but the two of us had known each other for a long time. He'd come by and say, "Hey, you doing anything tonight? Let's eat together."

Working with kids nowadays, I'll talk about hitting and invariably, I'll think of something Williams said or something he did as a hitter. There are times, I feel, the player is thinking, "Why is he talking about Williams?"

Ted was the greatest hitter I ever saw. Things that man did with a bat still stick in my mind. In 1957, for example, I saw Williams with the Red Sox make another run at .400. At 38, he batted .388! In the '46 All Star Game, I was on the team but Williams just stole the show from everybody. Teddy went 4-for-4 with two home runs. He hit a knuckleball off of Kirby Higbe and then hit Rip Sewell's blooper pitch.

While I was with the Red Sox, the manager was Pinky Higgins, one of my idols as a kid. An uncle of mine got me interested in baseball by taking me to games in Philadelphia, seeing the old Philadelphia A's when Connie Mack managed them. I cheered for the A's, especially for Higgins, Jimmy Foxx, Lefty Grove and Al Simmons. My favorite player, though, was Charlie Gehringer of Detroit.

When I broke in with the Senators, Higgins was playing for the Tigers. When I joined the Red Sox, he reminded me of a play my rookie season. Higgins couldn't imagine why I'd be playing in for a bunt with him up there. I thought Pinky was going to lay one down because Detroit had men on first and second with no outs. He just wheeled around and hit a shot right at me. I caught the ball, tagged first base and threw to second to complete a triple play.

For me, first base was an easy position to play. It is a position where you know you're going to be involved in a number of plays during a ballgame. I played the outfield my first year in Legion ball. The following year, they moved me in to first base. One of my teammates in Chester, Pennsylvania, was Danny Murtaugh. We lived about two miles from one another.

When I turned 17, I tried out for an oil refinery team in my hometown and showed enough to make the grade. They were all a bunch of older fellows who worked at the plant. I was playing against a good class of players and that just improved my play. This is where, I think, I started attracting the attention of scouts. A couple of them came by the house and spoke to my dad. One fellow talked to me about going to college. That was Doc Jacobs who was the baseball coach at Villanova and he offered me a scholarship.

Truthfully, I wasn't really prepared for college. I went to a vocational high school and Doc could sense that I wasn't coming back for my second year at Villanova because my grades weren't too hot. I wanted to play pro ball and if things didn't work out, I'd go back to Marcus Hooks and maybe find a job at one of the refineries.

Jacobs felt I had a chance to play at the pro level and he took me to Philadelphia, the first trip the St. Louis Browns came to town. Doc, you see, needed players for a team he was going to manage in the Eastern Shore League that summer. St. Louis did offer me a contract with a slight bonus. When I say slight, it was just that—about $1,000 on a contingent basis. If the parent Browns picked up my contract at the end of the year, I would get the bonus.

Bill DeWitt, who was running the St. Louis franchise, came to Easton during the summer. Bill evidently didn't think there was much talent on our ballclub because he didn't pick up mine or anyone else's option. That made me property of the Easton club and Jacobs wound up selling my contract to the Salisbury team in the same league. That's how I got into the Washington organization.

I played in the Sally League in 1938 and the following year, I went to Springfield in the Eastern League. I was leading the league in batting at .343 and on July 8, the Senators called me to the big leagues. I joined the ballclub in Philadelphia and because I lived so close to Philadelphia, I never bothered to call anybody at home. I wanted to see if my folks would hear my name on the radio. It would be kind of a surprise.

That day, the Senators were playing a doubleheader against the A's. I was late getting to the ballpark because my train connections from Springfield were fouled up. I eventually arrived at Shibe Park but the first game had already started. I dressed as fast as I could and got into the game as pinch-runner. In the second game, I played and went 1-for-4.

In my first at bat in the big leagues, I got a hit off Lefty Grove, which was quite a thrill, you know. As a youngster, I used to go to the ballpark to see him pitch.

Bucky Harris was a good manager in my estimation. He knew how to evaluate talent but it was just an unfortunate thing that he never had an awful lot of it around to be a contender. He managed early when he was the "Boy Wonder" and the great Walter Johnson was pitching for him. They won the pennant in '24 and '25 but he never did come up with that kind of a team again. Harris was a little sarcastic if you made a bad play. He wouldn't chew you out, just give you a cutting remark to let you know you made a mistake. He managed to let me have a couple of zingers and it sunk in.

The Senators were a veteran team with people like Sam West, Taft Wright, George Case, Buddy Myer and Ossie Bluege but they were looking for a first baseman. They had traded Joe Kuhel two years before for Zeke Bonura. When I arrived, Zeke was already gone. Washington was using a young fellow by the name of Jim Wasdell but he wasn't doing too well. Bluege played a few games over there before, I guess, Bucky decided to give me a try.

I eventually became a regular for the Senators until I joined the Navy in 1943. Washington had a chance for the pennant one year I was gone but lost it on the last day of the season. I can recall reading about Bingo Binks who dropped a fly ball in center field against Philadelphia because he didn't have his sunglasses on. The guys had all their gear packed to go to Detroit for the playoff game, too.

I didn't see any combat in the war but I did play a little baseball. The Navy formed two teams and we had several major leaguers in the ranks including Johnny Mize, Virgil Trucks, Pee Wee Reese, and Johnny Rigney. We traveled around to play for the servicemen, staying a month or so at each base. After the tour which ended in Guam, we were assigned to duty. I drew a place called Ulithi on the western Carolines in the South Pacific. I spent about 10 months there.

After the war, I don't know what happened to me as a player but I wound up hitting .353, the best I ever hit and I edged Williams for the batting crown. The two of us were taking turns leading the league. It was tight for awhile. I was lucky that it wasn't very close right down to the wire because Williams may have caught me.

Washington dealt me to Cleveland along with Early Wynn for Eddie Robinson, Ed Klieman and Joe Haynes after the 1948 season. The Indians had just won the pennant and it was an entirely different feeling in the clubhouse. They expected to win. Bob Feller and Bob Lemon headed quite a pitching staff and they had the offensive support with guys like Joe Gordon, Lou Boudreau, Ken Keltner and Larry Doby.

I didn't stay too long in Cleveland and I'll tell you what I think happened. I had a pretty good year, batting .291 with 83 RBIs, but the Indians didn't repeat as champions and were looking to move in some younger players. They had a big guy out in San Diego who was hitting a lot of home runs by the name of Luke Easter. They were priming him for first base.

I got the word real early when we were negotiating my contract. Hank Greenberg, who was the general manager, asked "Mickey, have you ever played the outfield?"

I told him I did in Legion ball.

"Would you be willing to try it?" he asked.

"I guess so if you'll maybe sweeten the pot," I said.

Hank started laugh.

"I remember when the Tigers did the same thing to you," I said. "They wanted to get Rudy York in the lineup and they moved you to left field and they gave you a little more."

"Mickey, we can't do that," he said.

Well, the season opened and Easter was in right field and I was playing first base. It wasn't too long before they started playing Luke at first because they found out he couldn't play the outfield. A day before the trading deadline, I was back with Washington in a deal for a young pitcher by the name of Dick Weik.

Washington improved itself with some trades, getting people like Jackie Jensen and Bob Porterfield. Porterfield won 22 ballgames for us in '53. To me, he just started to make good pitches. Bob always had the stuff and a good arm but it seemed his location was better and he started to get people out.

That year, I again led the league in batting but if the season went a little longer, Al Rosen might have passed me. He was shooting for the Triple Crown and he was coming on fast in September. Al was getting a lot of hits and gaining on me but I had a good cushion and he fell shy by a point.

Playing in Washington, I got to meet some of the politicians. Happy Chandler, for instance, would come in the clubhouse and greet the guys by their first name, chat and talk baseball. Happy was the former commissioner of baseball, you know. There were others too, like that fellow in Idaho, Senator Herman Welker, who recommended Harmon Killebrew to our ballclub. Senator Welker was around all the time. He also knew the game.

On Opening Day in '54, I had one of my biggest thrills in baseball. It was a custom that the President of the United States throw out the first ball to get the American League season officially started. Well, it was nice day in Washington and the game went into into extra innings.

Allie Reynolds, who came on in relief, hadn't been in there long. In the 10th, I guess Eddie Yost got on base and the next batter failed to bunt him over. I hit the next pitch over the right-center field fence to end the game. As I circled the bases, the players came up to home plate like they usually do to congratulate you. I touched home plate and there's one guy in civilian clothes there. He grabs me by the arm and says, "Mickey, I'm with the Secret Service. The President wants to see you." The two of us head over to the stands. President Eisenhower shook my hand and said, "That was a nice job. Congratulations." The photographers took several pictures and we chatted a little bit.

I had spent my whole career in the American League and I finished up with two teams in the National League, Milwaukee in 1959 and Pittsburgh in 1960. I reported to the Braves because, the more I started thinking, they had won a couple of pennants and I might have a chance to finally play in a World Series. We came close in '59 but at the end of the year, I was released.

Back home, Danny Murtaugh gave me a call and we went golfing. He asked me what I was going to do and I really didn't know. I felt I could still play, maybe pinch-hit for someone.

"Why don't you come with me as a coach," Danny said.

And that's what I did. I batted a few times for the Pirates and I finally got to a World Series.

Against the Yankees, we really got whacked around by those football-like scores in the Series, you know, 12-0 and 18-3, but our guys wouldn't sit around and moan or feel sorry for themselves. Tomorrow was another day and the guys came back the next day. They kept coming back and the seventh game was tomorrow for them. It was a crazy game and a wacky series because the Yankees scored more runs in winning three games than we did in winning four. But we scored more in the game that counted.

I would have liked to have been like Bucky Harris and manage 30 years in the majors but it just didn't happen. That's why it was quite a surprise when I got a call from Elwood Quesada, the fellow who was putting together the new expansion team in Washington. The old Senators moved to Minnesota and the American League added new teams in Washington and Los Angeles. We ended up with a few more older guys. The Angels found some good young players like Jim Fregosi, Bob Rodgers and Dean Chance. We had a .500 record for our first 60 games which took us right up to the June 15th trading deadline. I think some of the guys were hoping they'd join Hal Woodeschick and Tom Sturdivant and get traded. We just had too many players who had seen better days and others who were fringe major leaguers. And personally, it was tough managing a team where I had been a teammate of some of the guys.

16

Bill
Monbouquette

*B*ill Monbouquette broke into the majors with the Red Sox and quickly emerged as Boston's most consistent starting pitcher while toiling annually for second division teams at Fenway in the early 1960s.

Born August 11, 1936, in Medford, Massachusetts, "Monbo" spent 11 years in the major leagues. He was steady and dependable—logging six consecutive years of at least 200 innings and 30 starts. He compiled a 96-91 mark with the Red Sox, the bulk of his 114-112 career ledger. His best season was 1963 when the right-hander posted a 20-10 record on a team which finished seventh. He is also one of a dozen pitchers in franchise history to pitch a no-hitter—1-0 at Chicago on August 1, 1962.

Monbouquette also pitched in three All Star Games and was the starting hurler in 1960. He also set an American League record for most strikeouts in a night game—17 versus Washington on May 12, 1961—which has since been broken. (It is presently held by Boston's Roger Clemens—20 versus Seattle on April 29, 1986.) Monbo slumped to 23-32 *in his final two campaigns in Fenway and was traded to Detroit on October 4, 1965, for outfielder George Thomas and infielder George Smith. He finished his playing career in 1968 after stints with the New York Yankees and the San Francisco Giants.*

Since retiring, Monbouquette has worked in baseball at the major league and minor league level, serving as the big league pitching coach for the New York Mets as well as a pitching instructor for several teams in the Yankees' chain. He is currently the pitching coach for Toronto's farm club in the Florida State League at Dunedin.

◆　　　◆　　　◆

I never saw the inside of Fenway Park until I signed with the Red Sox. As a kid, I watched most of my big league baseball in Braves Field. I was a member of the Knothole Gang. We sat way up in the left field pavilion and the players looked like ants.

All the kids in the neighborhood dreamed of wearing a big league uniform. Probably the biggest reason I ever played major league baseball was because of Gus Hennessey. He was a friend of mine, almost like a second father to me. Gus was always the guy who kept saying, "Go with the fastball." That's what got me to the big leagues and that's what kept me there.

Baseball is a hard game but that's the way you have to play it. You're not going to have instant success. It just takes a willingness to pay the price and good work habits. Running was one thing I faithfully did because I enjoyed it. When I was the pitching coach with the Mets in 1983, I asked Tom Seaver one day if he liked to run.

"Not one bit," he said, "but I have to."

I think that's one reason why Seaver pitched as long as he did. The preparation he had before a game and the work he did after a game was great to see. You wish it would rub off on the younger kids because hard work pays off. Maybe some day when some of these kids in the minor leagues reach the big leagues, they'll look back and say, "The old Frenchman was right."

The big thing kids must learn not to accept is "I can't catch a break." You make your own breaks. I happened to be at Minneapolis in 1958 when Willard Nixon hurt his arm. I happened to be the youngest guy there and had the best record on the ballclub and so the Red Sox took a shot. Maybe they felt they weren't going anywhere so management decided to see what I could do. I tried to take advantage of it.

I had problems like every young pitcher. I wasn't with the Red Sox very long when I got summoned to the general manager's office. We had just returned from a road trip and I had been pitching pretty well. I was wondering what this meeting with Joe Cronin was going to be about.

"Mr. Cronin," I said, "you wanted to see me."

"How many times do I have to tell you, don't call me Mr. Cronin. Call me Joe," he said. Then he said, "Do you know how many years I've been in baseball?"

"Oh, I know it's a long time," I said.

"Well, let me tell you something. I have never seen anybody like you. Do you like playing in the big leagues?"

"Yes, sir. That's the only place to play."

"Do you want to go back to Minneapolis?"

"No, sir."

"Well, you better stop arguing every other pitch with the umpire."

Besides umpires, I also had my share of arguments with Mike Higgins. One year with the Red Sox, I can remember we were playing the Orioles in one of those crazy type of series where it ended on a Saturday. I wasn't due to pitch until Monday but Baltimore was the only club I hadn't beaten all season.

I went to see Sal Maglie, the pitching coach. "Sal, can you ask Mike if there is a chance for me to pitch against Baltimore?"

Maglie went in and convinced Higgins I should pitch. That day, I didn't get anybody out in the first inning, the first time that ever happened in my career.

Right after the game, we left for Detroit. At the hotel, I was coming downstairs to have my bags sent up to the room. I ran into Higgins in the elevator and he started to get all over me.

"Who do you think you are telling me when you want to pitch?"

I told him he could have said no and I wouldn't have complained.

The words led to a pushing-and-shoving match. The two of us were going at it pretty good. When the elevator landed in the lobby and the doors opened, suddenly, the writers are standing there. Naturally, they want to know what is going on. Higgins explained that we just had a difference of opinion and that was it. You know, nothing was ever said after that.

Higgins always went to bat for me. I enjoyed playing for him. It wasn't a situation where I couldn't play for the man or I wanted to be traded. I just went out there and did the best job I could.

I learned more about pitching from Ted Williams than anybody. Listening to him, I understood how a hitter thinks. He's the only guy I ever played with that if you got him out in the first inning, he'd say, "I'm going to hit that slider. It will be the third pitch in the seventh inning." And Williams would do just that! He was truly amazing.

Ten years ago, I probably would have said Williams, if he was playing, would hit .400. Today, because you don't see that many good curveballs, he might hit .500. Nowadays, everyone is down to the fastball syndrome. Hardly anybody pitches inside.

Very rarely did Williams get knocked down but this one time in Chicago, Turk Lown threw a ball behind Ted and sent him to the dirt. On the next pitch, Williams hit one right up the middle and the ball missed tearing off Turk's leg. When I took the mound in the bottom of the inning, I just literally flattened the first guy up. When the side was out and we were back in the dugout, Williams came by and said, "Thanks, Monbo."

I'd like to have $100 for every time Jackie Jensen said, "I'm going on my butt now." Jensen would say that after someone hit a home run. Knockdown pitches are part of the game because a pitcher has a right to the plate, too. Some kids aim the ball in there instead of throwing with some authority. A pitcher has to pitch inside with power, almost to the point where a hitter says, "Whoa, what's this?"

I don't believe in pitching inside for strikes. You can try to set up a hitter but if you are going to make a living, you have to pitch bad inside. A pitch close to the hitter is a lot easier to hit because he can turn on that ball. I'd run two balls in a row inside to prevent the hitter from getting comfortable up there.

Sometimes you'll hear someone say, "I see the ball good" or "I feel comfortable up there hitting off you." Well, you better do something about it. Maybe add some deception to your motion so the hitter can't pick up the ball. I remember in spring training one year when Williams was still playing. We'd fool around in intrasquad games and I'd try to fool him. I'd normally stand to one side of the slab but against Williams, I'd move down a bit. And Ted would start yelling, "Monbo, what the hell are you doing out there?" All I was trying to do was throw off his concentration and he didn't like it one bit.

My years in Boston, we had good hitters like Jensen, Pete Runnels, Frank Malzone and Carl Yastrzemski but we didn't have the double play combination. Consequently, during the course of a game, you ended up pitching that extra two or three innings. That's what kind of hurt. What you do is just go out there, do the best you can and battle as long as you can.

One thing we did have in Boston was the greatest relief pitcher I saw in my time. Dick Radatz came right in and just blew people away. He never took the cart to come into the ballgame. His motive was to let that hitter think about what he was going to face. Radatz came after you. The guys on other clubs used to talk on the bench, like, "Get ready to crank it up another notch," but that just didn't do any good. There was nothing tricky about Radatz. He just said, "Here it is."

I remember one instance in Fenway. I was beating the Yankees 1-0 and in the ninth inning, there was an error, a walk and a base hit. The Yankees had the bases loaded with Roger Maris, Yogi Berra and Johnny Blanchard due to hit. Johnny Pesky took me out and in came Radatz.

"I'll get them for you," he said.

I could see Radatz striking out Maris and Blanchard but Yogi was another type of hitter altogether. I got Berra only once in my career and that was a 3-2 pitch with the bases loaded on a ball up over his head. Well, Radatz struck out the three of them on nine pitches. He was just remarkable.

Probably the greatest thing that ever happened to me was the day I pitched the no-hitter against the White Sox. I always used to say when I went back to Chicago, I was back at the scene of the crime. For a no-hitter, a pitcher needs a little luck.

You can pitch well but make one mistake and you can lose the no-hitter and the game, too.

One time, I pitched two complete games in a week and managed only a split. That's the way it goes. I pitched a two-hit shutout against Minnesota and in my next start, also against the Twins, I had a perfect game going. I had two outs in the eighth inning when there was a ground ball to Malzone. He threw it over to Tony Horton and the ball went through Tony's legs. Tony Oliva was the next hitter. I had him two strikes and he fouled off nine balls, not strikes. I threw down and away, even sidearm but Oliva fouled off pitch after pitch. I tried coming up again and Oliva hit it out of the ballpark for a home run.

I finished my career with the Giants. In spring training, I remember playing in a "B" game at 10 o'clock in the morning. Some of the guys begged to get out of the lineup because Juan Marichal was pitching. He was truly a great pitcher, whether it was 10 a.m., two in the afternoon or eight o'clock at night.

Marichal, Bob Gibson, and Whitey Ford are probably the best I saw in my time in the big leagues but the guy who impressed me the most was Warren Spahn. He was pitching effectively when he was into his 40s! What he did, I don't think anyone will ever match. When you look up and find out his age when he first came to the big leagues and realize he wound up winning 363 games, that's tremendous.

85

17

Chet
Nichols

*F*or Chet Nichols, it wasn't difficult to figure out what to do as a youngster. Growing up in Rhode Island in the 1940s, his father, Chet Sr., who had pitched in the National League from 1926 to 1932, was more than just a tutor.

Chet Jr., born February 22, 1931, in Providence, broke in with the Boston Braves in 1951 and pitched just enough innings to lead the National League with a 2.88 earned run average. In his first three seasons with the Braves, who departed Boston for Milwaukee in 1953 and became a potent force later in the decade, Nichols compiled a 29-27 record.

But a two-year hitch in the military left the southpaw with chronic arm trouble, forcing him to quit in 1958. After sitting out a summer, Nichols made a comeback, and by 1960 he was back in the majors as a reliever. In a tad over three seasons with the Boston Red Sox, Nichols won five of 13 decisions and saved six games. He finished with a career record of 34-36, retiring after toiling for the Cincinnati Reds in 1964.

He is now a pitching instructor in the minor leagues for the Baltimore Orioles organization.

◆   ◆   ◆

Ever since I can remember, I had a baseball in my left hand. Maybe I was a disturbed child. My father had total influence on me and taught me more about pitching than most fathers. As it turned out, as the old saying goes, I was in the twilight of a mediocre career.

By my junior year in high school, I was developing into quite a pitcher and had a number of scouts looking at me. At the time, I had all intentions of going to college after a year of prep school at Moses Brown in Providence.

During my senior year, I changed my mind. I wanted to sign to play professional baseball. I did not have a great year and lost a couple of tournament games which backed off most of the scouts. But Jeff Jones of the Boston Braves, who went to all my games and was the scout who signed me, always made the same offer.

I signed a three-year major league contract because my father didn't want me to be a bonus ballplayer. At the time, my dad didn't feel that it would be best for me to go to the majors as a $25,000 bonus baby and not develop. The next best thing was a major league contract. I signed for $5,000, but I was guaranteed to be in the organization for three years.

Because I had signed a major league contract, I got a chance to go to spring training. The Braves had just won the pennant in '48 and it was a great experience. Evansville of the Triple-I League was my first stop and Bob Coleman was my manager. I think the first game I pitched there, I lost 1-0 and struck out 10 or 11 men. The next game, I lost 2-1 and struck out 12. I lost a couple of more times before I finally started to win. I finished the year at 14-and-7 on a team which won the pennant. We had a good team, too. Johnny Logan, Peter Whisenant, Del Crandall, and Eddie Mathews. Crandall, in fact, went up to the big leagues halfway through the year.

After a year in Milwaukee, I made the varsity. I was coming off a 7-and-14 year in the American Association, yet the Braves kept me in '51 because they needed a lefty and I was there. Just to be part of the team was a fantastic feeling. Here I was, a 20-year-old rookie and in the big leagues.

My main objective was to get along with the other ballplayers, go out and have a winning year with a good earned run average. One of the greatest compliments I heard was from Walker Cooper. He thought I could be another Warren Spahn.

I didn't do any pitching the first month of the season and was getting a little impatient but Johnny Sain gave me the best advice. I was going to ask to be shipped down so I could pitch. Sain said, "If you win one game in the big leagues, it's better than winning 10 or 12 in the minor leagues." And Sain was right.

My first win came against the Giants in the second game of a doubleheader at Braves Field. We lost the first game 8-7 or something and the second game was another high-scoring one. It was 8-8 and Billy Southworth ran out of pitchers. I was the only one left in the bullpen. I wound up pitching three innings and ended up winning the game.

Over the second half of the season, I got to pitch every fourth or fifth day and wound up getting enough innings to win the ERA title, edging Sal Maglie. Can you believe it? Me edging a pitcher like Maglie? I believe Jim Turner, who also pitched for the Braves, was the only other rookie to do that.

I beat one of the best pitchers in one of the better games I pitched that year to help knock the Dodgers out of the pennant race. Preacher Roe was 22-3 that year and I beat him, 3-2. Brooklyn had to go to Philadelphia next, needing to win to stay in the race. Then Bobby Thomson hit that home run to decide the pennant.

I spent 1952 and 1953 in the Army and when I came out of the service, I wasn't in shape. I joined the Braves in spring training and that's when I hurt my shoulder. It was my own fault in certain respects because I was a little heavy. The Braves were looking for me to carry on what I did my rookie year and that was one of the reasons why they made a deal with the Giants involving Johnny Antonelli and Don Liddle.

I reported in the middle of March and was behind everyone. They tried to get me in shape pretty quick but I didn't have the strength in my arm like before. I ended up going 9-and-11 but my shoulder was really bothering me. It got so bad that after a couple of seasons, I left baseball for a year.

I came back in 1959 because of Gene Mauch. He was the manager in Minneapolis and we had played together with the Braves. Neil Mahoney, the minor league director of the Red Sox, came down to watch me throw in a gym. I was throwing pretty good but you really can't tell because you're only throwing for 20 minutes and it's not facing a guy with a bat in his hands. You're not trying to break a curve a little better or pump up on your fastball.

I went to the American Association and did pretty well. I won a few games and pitched in the All-Star Game which was played in Minneapolis because the Millers had won the league championship in '58. I wound up winning the MVP trophy which wasn't too bad considering I had been out of baseball for a year.

The next year, I went to Vancouver and won 18 games. For the first time in a long time, I felt no pain throwing a baseball. I got my rest and worked every four or five days. George Bamberger was on the same club and he won 13 games that year. The Yankees were interested in buying my contract but the Red Sox wouldn't sell me and ended bringing me back to the big leagues.

With the Red Sox, I was used in relief or as a spot starter. That role was a little tough because my arm wasn't in shape for that type of pitching. I'd warm up a little and then sit down. I'd throw a little more and again sit down. My arm would stiffen and I never reached my potential. The problem was my arm.

In my day, the philosophy was to have a pitcher go nine innings. No team had a long man in the bullpen. A starter like Spahn would give up four or five runs and still be in the ballgame. He was a better pitcher tired and giving up four runs than anyone else who was available. To me, Spahn was one of the finest pitchers in the major leagues. At one time, he had a great fastball and a good curveball. As he got on in pitching, he developed a screwball. What a competitor he was! Some say the generation of players I played with enjoyed baseball more than today's players because we never got paid that much. I don't know if that was the reason. In my day, there seemed to be more compatibility because you had more players in an organization and guys went up together. You had to pay your dues. Johnny Sain, for example, spent eight years in the minors. I was fortunate to get up there in three years on a veteran team. The Braves had something like 300 guys in their organization. Today, every team has about 100 players.

If you look at the '50s and the teams, you'll hear some old-timers say that the ballplayers today can't play. Comparing eras is like comparing fighters. It's what happens at a particular time. There are too many "ifs" in sports. The athletes today are better, but baseball, I believe, has lost a lot of talent to the other sports like basketball and track. Look at the way pro football has grown. You have to figure baseball has lost a few athletes somewhere.

I do know I played against some great players. The Braves were always chasing the Dodgers and the Giants. We either finished second or third. Brooklyn had Roy Campanella, Jackie Robinson, Pee Wee Reese, Carl Furillo, Duke Snider, Carl Erskine, Don Newcombe, and Preacher Roe. We weren't too bad with Henry Aaron, Eddie Mathews, Johnny Logan, Joe Adcock, Del Crandall, Andy Pafko and Billy Bruton. The Giants hit so many homers and they had a pitching staff with Sal Maglie and Larry Jansen. The more you look at it, there were strong clubs right down the line. Each team had depth. There were more people in the system because there were more ballplayers available.

We had some characters in Milwaukee. Spahn was a funny guy. Lew

Burdette, my roommate, was another. I played with Bob Uecker. There's a comic for you. Uecker couldn't hit or throw and everyone wondered how he got to the big leagues. Charlie Grimm was another. He used to play a banjo in the clubhouse. When he was our manager, we had about two signs. "Just go up there and make sure you swing the bat." That was Charlie. He'd let you go out and play, one of those, "Here's the ball and gloves, now go get them, gang" types.

I'll tell you how great an athlete Aaron was. As a rookie, he weighed only 165 pounds. We were in Philadelphia and Curt Simmons was pitching. I was sitting next to Mathews on the bench and Simmons threw an outside fastball that Henry hit over the right-center field fence for a home run. Eddie just shook his head. For a left-handed hitter, Mathews had all he could do to hit them out in right. Aaron had great wrists. If you talk to the opposing catchers, they were ready to catch the ball and swoosh—here came the bat. That's how quick Henry was.

If I had reacted quicker, I might have caught a historic home run, the last one ever hit by Ted Williams. In his last at-bat at Fenway, all of us in the Red Sox bullpen were trying to kill each other for the baseball. Williams was amazing. He did everything you had to do to be a great hitter. I still say, if Ted could crawl to the plate, he could hit. Even up until the time he retired, Ted still swung the bat with authority. His numbers, if you check the records, are right up there. You wonder what they would have been if he didn't spend time in the service.

I saw Roger Maris break Babe Ruth's record, too. I relieved Tracy Stallard after Roger hit his 61st home run. Maris was hitting again and could have hit 62. Maybe I should have thrown it. After the game that day, some guy knocked on the clubhouse door and wanted one of Stallard's gloves. The guy said, "I'll give Stallard $1,000 for the glove he used." Tracy had three or four in his locker. He grabbed the closest one and handed it to that fellow in a hurry.

18

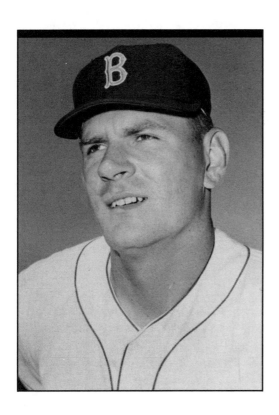

Dick
Radatz

*I*n *the early 1960s, the Red Sox had a "Monster" in the bullpen. An imposing figure who wore size 14 shoes to support his six-foot-six and 240-pound frame, Dick Radatz was a hard thrower who played a significant role in 149 of 286 Boston wins over a four-year period.*

From 1962 to 1965, Radatz delivered a steady diet of fastballs in the high 90s against which opposing hitters, well aware of what was coming, found themselves overmatched. Striking fear in many a hitter, Radatz emerged as one of the premier relievers in baseball, twice being named to the American League's All-Star Team.

Although the Red Sox were consistent also-rans during his tenure in Boston, Radatz performed admirably. As a 25-year-old rookie, he logged 62 appearances, posted a 9-6 mark with 24 saves and a 2.24 ERA. In 66 games in 1963, the right-hander went 15-6 with 25 saves. In 1964, he went 16-9 with 29 saves in 79 games. When Radatz slumped to 9-11 with 22 saves in 1965 and began having control problems and losing velocity, the Bosox eventually dealt away their stopper to Cleveland for Don McMahon and Lee Stange on June 2, 1966.

Within three years, Radatz was gone from the big leagues. He finished his seven-year stay with a composite 52-43 record, 122 saves and a 3.13 ERA. His 381 appearances also included stops with the Chicago Cubs, Detroit Tigers and Montreal Expos. Radatz's 745 strikeouts in 693 2/3 innings makes him one of a select few to average more than a strikeout per inning during a major league career.

◆   ◆   ◆

Earl Wilson likes to tell this story. Earl says he had a tendency to look out toward the bullpen, especially in the late innings, knowing I was out there to save a win for him. I believe this was in 1963. We're playing the Yankees, and Fenway is jumping, a full house, like any time the Red Sox and Yankees go at it. That night, Wilson is pitching a heck of a game. He has a 2-1 lead going into the ninth but walks the bases loaded. There are no outs and waiting to hit are Mantle, Maris and Ellie Howard.

Johnny Pesky heads to the mound and asks Wilson how he's feeling. As Earl tells it, the only noise he and Pesky can hear above the crowd is my fastball hitting the catcher's mitt in the bullpen. Wilson is quite sure Pesky is going to take him out but he says, "John, I feel pretty good." Pesky gives him a pat on the butt and says, "Okay, Tiger. Go get 'em." At that point, Wilson says he nearly fell off the mound. He stops Pesky in his tracks. "Maybe I do feel a little tired. Let's get the big guy in here."

I get to the mound and Earl hands me the ball.

"Partner," he says. "Don't take too long or your beer will get warm."

"Don't worry," I said. "I'll be right in."

I struck out Mantle, Maris and Howard on ten pitches to save it for Earl. I got so pumped up about it, I wound up throwing my hands up over my head and the crowd went wild.

The next day, Curt Gowdy, who was broadcasting Red Sox games back then, sees me. He says, "Richard, do you realize what you did last night?"

"Yeah. I struck out Mantle, Maris and Howard."

"Not that. You threw your hands up over your head."

"I did?"

"The fans loved it. Why don't you keep doing it?"

That's how that victory salute started. It became my calling card.

Pitching in Fenway Park never bothered me. The Wall evened itself out. Killebrew would come in here and hit those 325-foot fly balls that would be outs in Minnesota but here, they're home runs. On the other hand, guys like Kaline would come here and hit balls off the top of the

Wall and wind up with singles. I never pitched with the Wall in the back of my mind. Once in a while, a short fly would get out of here and that would bother me, but there were other times the hitters ripped a line drive and I said a little prayer of thanks that the Wall was there.

I had never been to New England before '62 but once I came here, I fell in love with the area. I grew up in Detroit, a blue-collar town. I was a Tigers fan but if I had to rate which sport I liked most, it would have been basketball. I went to Michigan State on a scholarship and thought I was John Havlicek. Turned out, I was more like Mrs. Havlicek.

Baseball was an after-thought until a couple of people woke me up and felt I had some talent. I then took the bull by the horns and did something about it. The Red Sox were one of several teams interested in me. Detroit, Baltimore and the Chicago White Sox had scouts at my games in college but the guy who signed me, Maurice DeLoof of the Red Sox, was the most fair and honest.

It was Pesky who decided to make me a relief pitcher in Seattle in '61. All my life I was a starter and had some success in my first two-and-a-half minor league seasons. But Pesky had this idea about using me in the late innings. At first, I thought it was a demotion. In those days, if you weren't good enough to start a game, they put you in the bullpen. Quite honestly, my rookie year in Boston, I didn't feel I was an intricate part of the ballclub even though I was the American League's Top Fireman with all those saves.

In my second year, I began to think different about it. At the time, several teams were developing a relief specialist. The Yankees had Luis Arroyo, Kansas City had John Wyatt. The Braves had Don McMahon and the Giants had Stu Miller. It was like the dawning of the relief pitchers, guys who were used strictly out of the bullpen. Konstanty, Page, and Face came a bit earlier, but for the most part, they began their big-league careers as starters before making a great career out of short relief.

As everyone knows, I was a one-pitch pitcher and probably threw 85 percent fastballs just to keep the hitters honest. Either hit it or get out. I literally thrived for that one-on-one confrontation. I had to have that challenge like I needed three square meals a day.

A century from now, the fastball will still be the best pitch because it requires a hitter to react the quickest and that's the hardest thing for a batter to do. In all team sports, the individual must perform. In baseball, a pitcher has to get the hitter out. In football, a lineman must pound that guy across the line. On the basketball court, a defender can't let his man find room along the baseline. To me, the pitcher-and-hitter rates as the greatest single showdown.

I feel fortunate that I was able to play professional baseball, but I have the utmost respect for the nine-to-five guy. The only difference between someone who punches the clock and what I was doing is that 50 million or so are enamored with baseball. The only difference between me and a person working at Data, United General or some other company, is that if we both did our job to the best of our capabilities, I got my name in the paper and he didn't.

What's tough, and some handle it better than others, is what happens when your playing career is over. You can't play forever but when you're in the game, you believe you will. The adjustment or lack of recognition is rough. People don't know who I am? Are they crazy? Can't they read?

The adjustment is difficult. Some completely go down the tubes. Some stagger for a while. It took me almost two years to come out of it and get on with my life. For all the discipline in baseball, it doesn't really prepare you for what happens after baseball.

When you're playing, everything is done for you. The hotel and plane reservations, the meals. All you have to do is be able to tell time, not miss the bus to the airport and perform on the field. Once you establish yourself and have some success, barring injury, you stay around for a couple of years. You are the man and your ego goes right along with it. All of sudden, one day, it goes away and you wonder what the heck happened.

I wish I had been able to develop another pitch because the day comes when the fast one goes south. When I started to bounce around like I did at the end of my career, it was tough. I went to Detroit, my hometown, and felt it would be nice to finish up there. The Tigers had a championship team and as a pitcher, I felt I was on the way back to where I once was. I had some trouble with my delivery but I felt I was back. For whatever reason, I was dealt to the Expos and it was then that I decided it was enough. I wanted to see my family grow up.

The only personal regrets I have with the Red Sox is that I had to leave and I thought it was a bit premature. But that's another story. The other is that we didn't win more games with the talent that we had here with people like Frank Malzone, Pete Runnels, Captain Carl, Tony C and on and on. The defense and starting pitching was a little shaky and we were mostly a second-division ballclub. It would have been nice to finish a little higher.

Red Sox fans have had plenty of tough times following their team but that period in Boston was probably tougher for us on the field. When you go into July and August and don't really have a chance to win, it really becomes a long year and a bit boring too, especially sitting in the bullpen some 400 feet away. All you're doing is playing for personal pride. Believe me, it's tough.

19

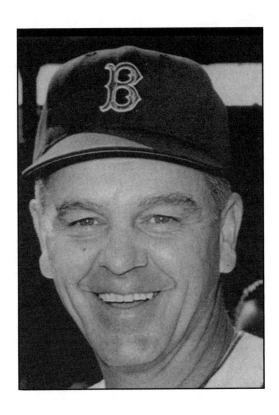

Dick Williams

*T*hough in his playing days Dick Williams failed to stir up Bean-town, few who were there will ever forget his debut as manager. By leading the Red Sox to the pennant in 1967, Williams shares with Jake Stahl and Ed Barrow the distinction of being the only rookie pilots to direct the Bosox to the flag. However, unlike the other two, Williams's Boston baptism is forever remembered as the "Impossible Dream."

Williams, born May 7, 1928, in St. Louis, spent 13 years in the big leagues, mostly as a reserve. He joined the Red Sox on December 10, 1962, in a trade with Houston involving outfielder Carroll Hardy. For two seasons, Williams appeared in 140 games before he went to manage in the minor leagues. With Boston's International League affiliate in Toronto, Williams directed the Maple Leafs to two consecutive Governor's Cups, a trophy awarded to the league champion.

Hired to direct the parent Red Sox, Williams inherited a team which had finished ninth the previous season. The cast included several who *had played for him in the minors. When October rolled around, the Red Sox won the American League pennant en route to their first World Series date since 1946.*

In three seasons in Boston, Williams had a .545 winning percentage. His success continued with other teams. Overall, Williams has managed over 3,000 games and has taken the Oakland Athletics and San Diego Padres to the World Series, winning consecutive titles with the A's in 1972 and 1973.

◆　　◆　　◆

They talk about expansion in the next decade and I dread to think about it. It would still be the best baseball that there is unless Japan got a little stronger. The good players—the Mattinglys, the Winfields, the Boggses—can excel in any era but some of the others belong in Double A. There were .210 hitters when I played too, but you didn't read about them because they hit .210. We also didn't make the bread like the players today are.

I was a young kid in 1929 when the market crashed. I know my dad was out of a regular job for about seven years but we were fortunate because my grandfather had a grocery store so we always had food on the table. You don't realize how tough things are when you're six or seven years old. My father didn't have the money to go out and buy me a pair of baseball shoes or a new ball. Like everyone else, when the cover came loose, we put electrician's tape over it. Once in a while, my father would get a ball for my brother and me because he used to umpire games at the Fairgrounds.

You had to like baseball growing up in St. Louis. We had the Browns and the Cardinals and Sportsman's Park was five blocks from our school. My brother and I were members of the Knothole Gang. We'd get out of class at 3:15 and get to the ballpark by the bottom of the first or the top of the second. In school, my favorite subjects were math and geography. Back then, you knew where all the countries were. Africa was Africa and Asia was Asia. You didn't have all the little nations or the name changes.

Here's a baseball geography lesson. I signed with Spokane, a farm club of the Brooklyn Dodgers. At the time, they had 29 teams in their system. You know I never saw Spokane until about six years ago because I happened to be going there.

I started as an outfielder but in my second year at Santa Barbara, in the California League in 1948, I injured myself pretty good. I had a three-way separation with my shoulder and collarbone. I had to get some pins put in and since it was on my throwing arm, it was from that point I couldn't throw worth a lick. But the Dodgers had a philosophy to find a position for a guy. They'd put an outfielder at second base. That was Branch Rickey's style.

The Dodgers were so loaded with talent that I wasn't the only one who couldn't find regular work. Preston Ward could play, but he had Gil Hodges ahead of him so Ward went to Pueblo in the Western League. Others would go down to Fort Worth in the Texas League. The competition made the guy on top, and the guys in Triple A and Double A, bust their tails because 20 other people were ready to take a job. You don't find that today because baseball no longer consists of 16 teams and because a lot of fabulous athletes are playing in the NBA or NFL.

In the Dodger organization, you learned the game the way Rickey told you to play it. They school you at Vero Beach in fundamentals so you learn to play a number of positions. Be versatile. You were also a number. It might be 85 orange or 64 green or 71 purple before they assigned you to a ballclub. We'd start at 8 a.m. and they worked us over on fundamentals until it was dark. It would be better than a week before we played a ballgame. The Dodgers fundamentaled the devil out of you and that has a way of sticking. Total repetition. You can tell a player a thousand times and nothing will happen. Maybe on the 1,001st try, it will.

If you ever manage in this game, you can't overlook the basics. You look up the team that usually won and you'll find they didn't make mistakes to beat themselves. You also look over the last three decades and check the ballplayers that became managers. Their lives touched Branch Rickey, either when he was with the Cardinals, Dodgers or Pirates.

Leo Durocher was a Rickey man for a long, long time. I learned more about baseball from Bobby Bragan in Double A, long before I reached the majors. Chuck Dressen, Eddie Stanky, Herman Franks, Al Dark, Gene Mauch, Walt Alston, Tommy Lasorda, Don Zimmer, Roger Craig, and Gil Hodges are some more old Dodgers.

I remember that spring training in '67 like it was yesterday. I had a strict program where we had to be working on things at a certain place and time. If I was going to go down, I was going to go down my way. I made up my mind to run that club the way I wanted to. Maybe that's why Ted Williams walked out of my camp.

I took the whole club, position-by-position, around the diamond, explaining offensive and defensive possibilities. It took three days to do it, a good hour-and-a-half at each stop. I talked about things like when to pick up signs. It starts in the on-deck circle. The sooner you look, the coach will flash a sign—even before you leave the batting circle.

We didn't have the luxury of an auxiliary field in Winter Haven, except for maybe extra hitting. We did have plenty of space in left field and

I wanted my outfielders to take balls off the bat. During batting practice, you tend to get pitchers who are not working that day, clustered in groups. They don't really shag, maybe interfere with the outfielders. So we set up a volleyball net and had the pitchers work out. I took a chance that someone would not get seriously hurt—say that a spike hit the tip of a finger. The pitchers had some games out there, too. There was some wagering, too, like for a case of beer or dinner.

When I was with the Red Sox, teams were beginning to groom pitchers for relief situations in the minors. John Wyatt was our stopper but we also had Sparky Lyle. In Oakland, the A's really didn't have a relief pitcher. Rollie Fingers was a starter when I went there in 1971. Rollie was such a hyper guy that as the days progressed to his next starting assignment, he would be a nervous wreck. The guy I give credit to for putting him in the bullpen was my pitching coach, Bill Posedel. "Maybe he can get his feet on the ground," is what Posedel said. We used Rollie in long relief and he did the job. Middle relief and he did the job. He may have pitched five or six times and then I put him in a save role and he saved the game.

What made everything go in Oakland was we also had Vern Hoscheit, a tremendous bullpen coach. He had our guys keeping up with the game as it progressed, such as what the possible changes are or tell me to back off about a pitching change because they have a righty coming up. Besides Fingers, we had Darold Knowles and Paul Lindblad. It was a time of lefty-righty or righty-lefty combinations in the bullpen.

With Montreal, Elias Sosa was our stopper. We also had a guy who later enjoyed some success. Don Stanhouse wasn't effective as a starter so I put him in the bullpen. When he went to Baltimore, Stanhouse had a couple of pretty good years. He worked slow, it was always three-and-two. The concessionaires had a booming business. Weaver called him "Six Pack" because Earl would smoke six packs of cigarettes every time he put Stanhouse in a game.

I think every manager can use a refresher course. Stay around long enough, you're bound to see just everything. Just before I left the Mariners, we were playing Detroit and I saw us turn a pitcher-to-catcher-to-third base doubleplay. All force plays. I managed a long time but I had never seen that before.

Steve Trout was pitching and Dave Bergman hits a line drive right back at him. The ball hit off Trout's glove and landed right in front of him. Trout threw home to Scott Bradley for the force and we were fortunate that there was a slow runner at second because we would have never gotten Bergman because he can scoot down the line. Bradley wisely went to third, a head's-up play on his part.

20

Jim
Lonborg

*T*here was a time in the early 1960s that Jim Lonborg put medical studies on hold to pursue a career in baseball. Few go back to college, but Lonborg, who helped trigger a pulsating pennant race for Red Sox fans, did and today, he operates a growing dentistry practice in Massachusetts.

Occasionally, a patient will ask Dr. Lonborg if he pitched for the Red Sox. Some go on to say that they were among the 35,770 at Fenway Park on the afternoon of October 1, 1967, when Lonborg beat Minnesota 5-3 to clinch the pennant, the first for Boston in 21 years.

It was an incredible year for Lonborg, who led the American League in victories with 22 and strikeouts with 246 and won the Cy Young Award. In the World Series against St. Louis, "Gentleman Jim" hurled the fourth one-hitter in the history of the Autumn Classic in Game 2, and then spun a three-hitter in Game 5. Working on just two days rest in Game 7, Lonborg lacked his usual zip and the "Impossible Dream" came to a close. Hall of Famer Bob Gibson throttled the Red Sox on three hits to post a 7-2 victory in the final game of the season.

◆ FENWAY VOICES

In 1968, Boston's pennant hopes were dimmed when Lonborg tore two ligaments in his left knee in an off-season skiing accident near Lake Tahoe. Following reconstructive surgery and therapy, Lonborg struggled to regain his effectiveness in his remaining tenure with the Red Sox. Besides knee trouble, tendinitis developed in his right shoulder.

Eventually, Lonborg was traded by the Red Sox to Milwaukee and then later by the Brewers to Philadelphia. During his 15 years in the majors, Lonborg compiled a 157-137 record with a 3.86 ERA despite a series of injuries. With the Phillies, Lonborg had a 75-60 record including an 18-10 campaign in 1976 when he again won a pennant-clincher. His victory on September 26th against Montreal ended a 26-year flag drought in Philadelphia.

◆   ◆   ◆

My wife always told me I looked good in a uniform and she was the one who first mentioned about becoming a dentist to me. After I was released by the Phillies in June 1979, my family and I just kind of relaxed and spent time together, casually discussing career possibilities. On a vacation trip to Vermont, she just happened to mention, "Why don't you think about becoming a dentist?" The more we discussed it and talked about it, the more viable an idea it became. Over the years, we made a number of friends in the Boston area and I started making phone calls to some who were dentists. I kept getting positive feedback. Within a couple of weeks, I made the decision. Going back to college, in a way, was kind of like going to spring training. I'm fortunate things have worked out. It seems you're just forever trying to pay back.

Like it was during my career in baseball, I'm doing something today that gives me a great deal of satisfaction. I look forward to going to work every single morning. I don't know what's going to happen every time a patient comes into my office. That provides a certain sense of the unknown challenge, much like you don't know what's going to happen every time you pitch a ballgame. From that standpoint, there's a lot of similarity. There's preparation involved in different cases, something you have to do in every profession. You have to be prepared, not only physically but mentally, for what lies ahead of you. You have to trust yourself with regard to whether the goals you're setting for yourself are attainable.

My life's had its ups and downs, like anyone else's, but life's setbacks are what teach you how to be a success. If you can't handle the setbacks, it becomes difficult to progress or get better. A college education, I think, helps you to handle the lows that everyone is going to encounter in the course of their careers. That's why young kids sometimes have difficulty, because they don't have the experience of college preparing them psychologically.

From pitching in college, I was prepared somewhat for professional baseball. The more you play, the more you become aware of what your skills are and what you can do. At an early age, my skills were good but not at a level that you'd say, "He's a natural." My folks emphasized academics because schooling would carry you through life. Sports was an outlet, something you could enjoy, relax and take up some of your time.

I studied biology in college and I'm not sure how that developed. It was just an interest I had. One of the reasons may have been the teachers I had in high school. They were instrumental in making it interesting and once you find someone that allows you to capture some of the excitement of nature, it becomes easier to pick up on.

My father was a professor. I was born in Santa Maria, California, but was raised in San Luis Obispo. It was a peaceful part of the state, halfway between Los Angeles and San Francisco. My wife and I truly love New England, but California might be one of the most beautiful states because of its diverse terrain. The Sierra Madre Mountains. Death Valley. The redwoods and sequoias. Just incredible country.

At Stanford, the coaches and scouts didn't know the level of my baseball skills. Basketball was my main interest because of my height and defensive skills. I guess you'd say I was a late developer physically. I didn't overpower a lot of people. I had good control and was able to maintain good mechanics. All of a sudden, I got stronger and baseball became a priority.

During the summers, I played in the Basin League, which was a collegian league that the Orioles had set up in Everett, Washington. The Baltimore organization heavily supported amateur baseball. The nice thing about the league was the fact that it was similar to the routine in professional ball. We played five or six games a week and had road trips.

One year, a competition developed between the Orioles and the Red Sox. The baseball draft hadn't been instituted yet and the Orioles, I guess, kind of assumed that I was going to sign with them because they had committed themselves to me but the Red Sox kind of snuck in there and made a much stronger offer.

At the time, both teams were not doing well. That is one opportunity to look at when you are entertaining thoughts about playing in the big leagues. I picked the Red Sox because they seemed to be in more need of pitching and I also had a feeling that I might get to the big leagues a little bit quicker if I signed with Boston.

It almost seems funny to say this but pitching in the big leagues was easier than any league I ever played in. It seemed you were not really doing anything different from what you did at each successive stage in the minors but conditions were great, the mounds were always immaculate and the defense was better.

When I came to Boston in 1965, the Red Sox were in a transition period with a lot of players. People like Eddie Bressoud, Chuck Schilling, Frank Malzone and Dick Radatz were finishing up at the same time the Red Sox were trying to develop a blend of young players. Boston had nothing to lose by developing this talent because they were near the bottom of the standings.

On most days, it was an adventure going out there because our defense, not to slight anyone, wasn't the greatest in the world. The year I went 9-and-17, Billy Herman told me that I could have been 17-and-9 if we had been blessed with a stronger defense. I was a sinkerball pitcher. Everything was being hit on the ground but no one could catch it. Staying out of the four-out innings can mean the difference between winning and losing.

In those days, what is also important to remember is the kind of fields we played on. They were mostly natural turf and teams could doctor up the field a bit. Wet down the area in front of home plate and maybe let the grass grow a bit longer. That combination can make it difficult for a hitter to drive the ball through the infield. Natural grass can be helpful to a sinkerball pitcher.

A lot has been said about our "Impossible Dream" but if you go back and look at how the Red Sox finished up at the end of '66, only one other team had a better second half than we did. We felt good about ourselves and the chemistry was mixing together. What helped more than anything, though, was the defense. In '66 and '67, Joe Foy, Rico Petrocelli, Mike Andrews and George Scott had arrived.

In the off-season, Dick O'Connell made a few good trades and hired a new manager. Dick Williams instilled a basic fundamental way to play baseball and stressed it to a point where he got everyone angry, riled enough of us to just worry about trying to catch the ball or throw it to the right base. His approach was to go out and play consistent, fundamental baseball. Make the routine play. Over the course of a season, 95 percent of the plays you have to make are routine ones.

Williams showed no favorites. Everyone was under his wrath. By the middle of the year, everyone basically knew their responsibilities. There may have been a carry-over feeling from the previous year but I think Williams saw something in us as a ballclub. With the pitchers, it was just throw strikes and don't walk hitters.

That season, we never had a chance to look very far ahead because the race was so close. Going into the last week of the season, Chicago had the best shot to win the whole thing. The White Sox had Joel Horlen and Gary Peters pitching on a Thursday night in a doubleheader against Kansas City, the worst team in the league. Horlen and Peters were two of the best pitchers that year. Both got beat by the Athletics and that just blew their chances. California and Detroit had two doubleheaders on the final weekend and we had to knock heads against Minnesota.

Jim Kaat was beating us 2-0 on Saturday and hurt his elbow. The way he was throwing that day, you know, we wouldn't have had a chance to beat him. All of sudden, he gets a sore arm, their bullpen comes in and we come back. I don't think anything will ever compare to the last day of the season. Not only was winning the pennant fun but it was done so many different ways with so many different styles and involved so many people.

It might have been a different story if I had three days rest before the seventh game, but you don't know whether you're going to score runs off Gibson. He was having an incredible year. What we accomplished as a team that year, I don't think most of us were able to understand the full impact until two or three weeks after the season.

The main problem in my recovery after the skiing accident was I was trying to throw too hard too soon. Somewhere along the line, I always felt like, if given the right set of circumstances, whether it was in conditioning or gaining strength in my legs, I knew everything was going to be all right. I really hadn't developed a great idea of what it took to get an arm back into shape again because of my exuberance to get back to the game. I had a normal program yet I was so anxious to throw hard, I overextended myself. There were setbacks in regard to the way my arm would recover after pitching, so it took me a good two or three years to figure out what I had to do to get myself to a point where my arm would be able to pitch the whole summer. I hurt my arm in '68, '69 and '70 at different times of the year. I was in the minors but came back to go 10 and 10 for the Red Sox. I started to pitch well again to a point, I felt, that 1971 was the best year consistency-wise that I ever had.

The Red Sox were making changes and I was moving on to Milwaukee. Getting traded the first time is always a shock. Each team tries to develop a sense of family within the organization. You're proud to be part of it and you work hard to represent yourself and the ballclub in a good manner. When you're traded, you wonder how the family could let you go. There was disappointment because I had finished up strong and felt I was on the road back.

I pitched only one year for the Brewers. At the time, Milwaukee was a first-class organization for a relatively young team. When I was traded to Philadelphia after the season, I realized the business in baseball but I was also joining a team that, on a bad day, would score four or five runs.

During my years with the Phillies, Dick Allen was the most awesome hitter I ever saw but Mike Schmidt, once he learned the strike zone, showed his true talent. Schmidt could put a charge in a ball, too, but he didn't have the kind of power Allen had. I've never seen anybody hit a baseball like he could. Dick would have those years in the National League where he'd hit .302 or .317 and strike out 150 times. You just had to be in awe when he wasn't hitting the ball hard somewhere. When Allen did, it would basically turn out to be a hit since there wasn't really any in-between for him in terms of what his talent was like. Jim Rice probably has comparable ability to hit the ball a long way but nobody could hit the ball farther, in all directions, than Dick Allen.

Steve Carlton was dominating every year I was with Philadelphia. We pitched against each other in Game 5 of the '67 World Series. All I can recall was that he was a tall, gangly kid who pitched a helluva ballgame that day. At the time, Steve wasn't the overpowering type of pitcher, in terms of strikeouts, that he developed into.

When you're playing baseball, you sometimes think your career is going to last forever. You always say to yourself that you should make plans for tomorrow but when the time comes, it is usually when you least expect it. When your career does end, it becomes difficult to find something that provides as much joy and satisfaction, but I think I have. I knew baseball wasn't going to last my whole life. It was an adventure and I'm glad I was part of it. I loved every moment in a big league uniform but now I'm in another profession that I'll be able to do for another 15 years. Every now and then, a patient will reminisce about my career. It's a nice feeling to be remembered.

21

Mike
Andrews

*A*s a rookie in 1967, second baseman Mike Andrews was part of the "Impossible Dream," but he is best remembered for another appearance in the World Series.

In 1973, as a member of the Oakland A's, Andrews was "fired" by owner Charlie Finley for two fielding mistakes against the New York Mets in Game 2. Commissioner Bowie Kuhn intervened and ordered Finley to reinstate Andrews. Ironically, the episode eased embarrassment for a future Hall of Famer whose misplay in center field enabled the A's to begin a rally and force extra innings.

Andrews spent a total of eight seasons in the major leagues including five summers in Boston—briefly in 1966 and then a mainstay until a trade to Chicago on December 1, 1970. The second sacker had a career .258 batting average with 66 home runs including a personal-high 17 in his Fenway finale.

Born in Los Angeles, Andrews signed with the Red Sox in 1962. Within four seasons, he reached the big leagues and formed a steady double play combination with shortstop Rico Petrocelli. At the plate, Andrews usually was at the top of the order.

Today, Andrews is chairman of the Jimmy Fund charity in Boston. "I'm just a small part of something that is working to help people," he says. "To me, it's as rewarding as my time in the major leagues. It's tough to call it work when you have plenty of volunteers giving their time and raising money to help the unfortunate."

◆   ◆   ◆

People have said a lot of things about Dick Williams, but he was good for my career, and by far the toughest manager I ever played for. He was a hard driver. I mean, he was nasty. A Doctor-Jekyll-and-Mister-Hyde type of person. Off the field, he was great. On the field, either he'd force you to quit or he'd get you so mad that you wanted to do the job in spite of him. His style served as a motivator for me and by the time each season ended, he had you saying, "Boy! Thanks a lot." But during the season, you were saying, "That no good so-and-so." That's really the story in 1967, the "Impossible Dream." It was a ballclub that had a lot of players who had never been treated in such a fashion, including Yastrzemski. Much has been said about Yaz and Dick Williams, that the two of them didn't get along, but you look at his career and see what Yaz did under Williams and compare it to what he did under everybody else, I think there's something there. Dick was the right guy at the right time for the Red Sox.

When Reggie Smith and I came up for the last part of '66, the two of us couldn't believe the attitude among the players. The team was so far out of the pennant race, I guess they were just glad to get the season finished. The year we won the pennant, our confidence level just grew week to week. In the beginning, no one expected us to win. By July, there was no team better in the league.

In '67, the players believed we were going to win. Yaz did anything that had to be done and the younger guys were used to winning championships in the minor leagues. At Toronto, we had won two straight Governor's Cups and Williams took a lot of us to Boston. Some of us had career years but my gut feeling was that the team had the makings of winning pennants for a number of years. . . but it never materialized. One of the major reasons we never did was Lonborg's injury. He was never the same pitcher after hurting his knee. The team never recovered after that. Changes followed and we started getting people who were at the end of their careers.

My career began when Joe Stephenson scouted me as a schoolboy in California. At the time, I played for Torrance High School and I didn't really know Joe until he approached me one day and asked if I would ever consider playing professional baseball. I had gone to a couple of tryout camps, including one held by the Pirates. They'd sit everyone down after a workout and then ask certain kids to stay. A couple of my friends were asked to remain and when the director came to me, he said, "Thanks for coming." I asked what I had to do to improve my game and he said, "Well. Speed-wise, you were pretty good. Your arm is above average. For a hitter, you swing the bat pretty good too. Son, why don't you stay for the game." I did and went 3-for-4.

I liked baseball but actually preferred football. I had a scholarship to play for UCLA, but before I could enroll, I had to attend junior college because I lacked a second year of a foreign language. I don't know if that's consistent with all colleges around the country, but to get into a state school one of the requirements was two years of a language. I had dropped a course to be the student body vice-president and looking back, that was one of the dumbest things I have ever done.

At El Camino Junior College, about six of us taking courses had major college football scholarships waiting. Baseball was something we could play as long as it didn't interfere with football. The coach was going to use me at first base because he already had a shortstop. When the opportunity to turn pro came along, I decided to sign.

My first year in pro ball was at Olean in the New York Penn League and there are two things I remember about it. In the second inning of home games, the umpires had to stop play because the sun would interfere with the game at sunset. I also recall the bleachers in right field. They were about 250 feet away from home plate and every time you hit the ball down there, it was an automatic double.

I played shortstop until my second year at Toronto. In fact, the Red Sox sent me to the Instructional League to learn how to play second. Rico Petrocelli was penciled in as their next shortstop. I found the adjustment rather easy. I had made my share of errors at short because of my delivery. I had relied on quickness to get rid of the ball, so really, the switch to second was made more for my ability. I didn't possess an overly strong arm but looking back, I didn't have the consistency to play the position. Once you have played shortstop, there is not a position on the field you can't play. Catching might be tougher to master but a shortstop, I think, can become a catcher more often than a catcher can become a shortstop.

Playing at Fenway Park, I started to pull the ball more and hit a few home runs. As a leadoff hitter, you have to be selective but also aggressive. Pitchers had to be careful because I did have some power and I think I hit three or four home runs to start a game but the point is, as a leadoff man, your job is to get on base. Look for a pitch you can drive and if you don't get it, a walk will also help the team. You can be aggressive but you also have to be smart. The more pitches you take, the more selective you become.

I really can't explain what happened to me in 1970 as a hitter. Eddie Kasko took over as manager and I had a terrible year at the plate. I hit .213 before the All-Star break and finished strong to wind up around .253 or so.

At the time, third base had become a problem for the Red Sox and the feeling in Boston was that they were going to make a trade. The idea about moving Petrocelli to third came about when Luis Aparicio of the White Sox became available. Boston had acquired Doug Griffin in a deal with the Angels and I had a feeling that I might be moving on. After the season, there was a newspaper article hinting that the Red Sox were going to make an offer for Aparicio. Dick O'Connell, the general manager, was quoted, "This is absolutely false. There is no way we would trade for Aparicio." That's the kiss of death. The next day, December 1, Luis Alvarado and I were wearing different socks. White ones.

The trade was the most disappointing time in my career. I had gone through the whole system with the Red Sox and all of a sudden, baseball wasn't really the same. I played with some great people in Chicago like Bill Melton, Ed Herrmann, Dick Allen and Wilbur Wood. Chuck Tanner was absolutely fantastic to play for, a real positive guy, but I just really never had the drive, the competitive fire like I did when I was in Boston. The first year, we played about .500 ball which was the worst year I've ever had in my life. The next season, Allen had a Yaz-like year and the only thing is we didn't win the pennant. We were leading the West until the last three weeks of the season. Oakland wound up sweeping five games from Detroit and we lost three of four to Texas. From that point on, it was all downhill.

With the White Sox, two youngsters, just out of high school, developed into a couple of good pitchers. Rich Gossage was just awesome and Terry Forster, at the time, actually had better stuff than Goose. Forster had a slider that was second to none to go with his fastball. The Sox were trying to make Goose into a starter. He could throw hard but couldn't last for nine innings. He was simply intimidating and his fastball was overpowering. The thing about both of them was their gutsiness. They were only kids and could throw close to 100 miles per hour and were not afraid to challenge the hitter.

Wilbur Wood was simply amazing to watch, about as amazing as watching people trying to hit his knuckler. He won over 20 games in each of the two years I was with the White Sox and he always kept you in the ballgame, a lot of ground balls. Sometimes, Tanner would use Wilbur to start both games of a doubleheader because the knuckleball didn't take too much out of him.

Yastrzemski could give the ball a good ride and I think Tony Oliva was the best hitter I ever played against. If Tony didn't hurt his knee, he would have eventually broken a few records. Oliva had a way of hitting the ball hard and you never knew where he'd try to drive it. You'd see his hands come through first but he wasn't always swinging flat-footed. You'd pray he'd hit you a nice, short one-hopper.

I don't think I saw anybody hit a ball harder than Dick Allen or Boog Powell. It was scary to be on the infield against either one because they hit the ball so hard. Allen and Yaz were the premier combination hitters I ever played with, but the hitter I always liked but never got to see that much of was Billy Williams because he was in the other league.

I finished my career with Oakland, and that came about because of Dick Williams. Williams called Charlie Finley because he felt I could help his club. Charlie was a pretty good judge of talent. Chicago was his home base so he saw me play a few times. He called me and said, "My manager wants you, but personally, I think you're all done." At the time, I was having a mental block about throwing the ball, something that Steve Sax had a couple of years ago. I played a few games but why it happened, to this day, I've never been able to figure out. Williams used me at second base but I was having a terrible time and had really lost a lot of confidence. I was being used strictly as a pinch-hitter. I may have played a few games at first base but I hadn't taken the playing field until the ninth inning of the second game of the 1973 World Series.

Finley was quite a character and the two of us almost went to court over what happened in the Series. I don't know the proper word to describe the type of owner that Finley was. A maverick? In today's game, he would not be as unique as some might think. Owners have done some unbelievable things. Ray Kroc used the ballpark public address system in San Diego to bad-mouth his team. George Steinbrenner has ruined a lot of young players in New York.

As everyone knows, in the 12th inning, I committed two errors on consecutive ground balls and it helped the Mets even the series. The next day, Finley decided to fire me and sent me home. Baseball Commissioner Bowie Kuhn stepped in and I was reinstated. I don't hold any bitterness towards Charlie but I think what he did was wrong. There is no place for that in this society, let alone in a sporting event so visible. The worst part of the whole situation was the state of mind that I was in, having this mental block about fielding. I had gone home and had left my house with the telephone ringing and just disappeared. I was getting telegrams from people all around the country. The players, who had a common dislike for Finley, were going to wear armbands on their sleeves with my number.

I can look back and laugh about it, but Finley had gone a bit too far.

111

◆ FENWAY VOICES

You know the weird thing about that game is that it was the last one Willie Mays ever played the field. He misjudged a ball hit by Deron Johnson and it helped us tie the game. I kid Willie about it now and then. I tell him, "I took you off the hook!"

22

George Scott

*G*eorge "Boomer" Scott, a husky first baseman who spent more than half of his 14-year career with the Boston Red Sox, called his home runs "taters." And Boomer hit his share of taters. In the field, Scott won more Gold Gloves—eight—than any other first baseman in American League history.

Born on March 23, 1944, Scott signed out of high school with the Red Sox. Boomer was 22 years old when he reached the big leagues in 1966, making the jump from the Double A ranks to full-time performer. Although Scott batted .245 and led the majors in strikeouts (152), he showed awesome power with 27 taters and 90 runs batted in.

On the "Impossible Dream" team, Scott batted .303—fourth highest in the league—and cracked out 19 home runs. The following year, his dropoff was worse than the Red Sox, batting just .171 with three homers and 25 RBIs. Scott's decline, however, did not last long. Boomer averaged 15 homers and 64 RBIs over the next three years before moving to Milwaukee in a 10-player swap on October 11, 1971.

With the Brewers, Scott had five productive seasons, his best in 1975 when he led the league in homers (36) and RBIs (109) while batting .285. On December 6, 1976, the Red Sox reacquired Scott along with outfielder Bernie Carbo for first baseman Cecil Cooper. At 33, Boomer fit right on a team which belted a club-record 213 homers including 33 during a 10-game spree from June 14 to June 24, 1977. Scott launched nine taters, including two to begin the streak and one to cap it. For the season, Scott slammed 33 homers, knocked in 95 runs, scored 103 runs and batted .269.

Injuries and increased calorie intake limited Scott's effectiveness in 1978 as his average dipped to .233. He began 1979 with the Red Sox, was shipped to Kansas City for outfielder Tom Poquette by mid-June, and eventually finished the campaign with the New York Yankees. Over his 2,034-game career, Scott slammed 271 homers and batted .268. In addition, he played in three All Star Games and slugged a two-run homer in the 1977 Classic.

Since retiring, Scott has managed in the Mexican League, helped organize recreational baseball leagues in his native Mississippi and also promoted baseball card shows.

◆   ◆   ◆

I go to games at Fenway Park from time to time and just walking through the doors, I get goosebumps, man. Just walking into the clubhouse... plenty of goosebumps.

Ever since I can remember, I wanted to play major league baseball. But where I come from down in Mississippi, they don't have a big program as far as baseball is concerned. Football is king but it's getting better. That's just the way things are. It takes time.

To this day, people back home tell me I was a better football player than baseball player. And I believe I was a pretty fair baseball player. I was just a good athlete. I enjoyed playing sports. Baseball, right now, is still fun for me. I enjoy working with the young kids. I like to see the youngsters progress. Maybe some day one can do the things I was able to do.

At Coleman High School in Greenville, I had 140 or 150 college scholarship offers. I could have gone damn near anywhere I wanted to go. I could have gone to UCLA. John Wooden scouted me to play basketball. I could play forward and also guard. It depended on what type of offense we ran. If it was a zone, I played guard and usually shot that zone down. I was averaging 35 points a game.

I had all the confidence in the world when I got to the big leagues. What really helped me get noticed with the Red Sox was the year I had in Pittsfield. In 1965, I was the MVP and won the Triple Crown. I hit .319 with 25 taters and 94 ribbys. Those are good numbers, no matter where you put them up. I can't forget that year or the great people in Pittsfield. Good memories, man.

The Red Sox have the greatest fans in the world. They were super to me.

The thing I remember most about Boston is Dick Williams. The man was fair and I appreciated it. Williams is a helluva man. You know, for me, he's always been one of my favorite people. We didn't always get along, yet I respect the man. He made me and he made our ballclub.

Dick Williams treated everyone the same way. He didn't give a damn if it was Yastrzemski or anyone else. If you did wrong, he got on you. Most ballplayers will tell you that's what they want the most. A fair chance. If they messed up, they want you to get on them. When someone else messed up, they want you to get on him, too. And Williams was that way.

Williams and I had a lot of run-ins, man, a lot of them, but I respected him because he was a fair man. As a person, athlete, or whatever, that's all you can go by. That's all that counts.

Williams had the ability to drive me to get the maximum. He called me names that I don't think were justified. I honestly think it wasn't his thought to try to harm me or hurt me but I wondered if he respected me as a player. Later on, I realized what he was doing. I hope he didn't take any of my actions personally. I still love the man because he motivated me. He made me realize that baseball is a dog-eat-dog game where people don't have a whole lot of compassion for you.

Everybody knows I agree pretty good with food. Williams and I disagreed quite a lot over my weight because of my tendency to eat. In '67, it came to a head in August when we were in Anaheim. We had an off day and there was nothing for me to do but eat. Before the game, Williams made me weigh in. I got on the scales and Williams watched me. I was 217, two pounds overweight.

"You're not playing," Williams said and he just walked away.

He benched me because I was two pounds overweight!

Man, I wanted to play. I wore those California pitchers out. I wanted to be in the lineup. I ran with a sweatsuit on to get the two pounds off and Williams still wouldn't let me play. You know, we lost each game in the series by one run. I guarantee that if Williams had to do it all over again, he would do it different.

I never wanted to leave Boston but I couldn't control that. The five years I was away, I believe I became a better player. I still hit my taters, but in the batter's box I was a more patient hitter. I didn't chase bad pitches.

◆ FENWAY VOICES

We didn't win much while I was with the Brewers. It was tough to come to the ballpark. Playing in Milwaukee, I did have an opportunity to spend two years with Henry Aaron, the greatest hitter in baseball history. Just to be around that man, in batting practice, at dinner, on the road, it made my eyes light up.

23

Lee
Stange

When used either in a starting or relief role, Lee "Stinger" Stange proved reliable, steady more than flashy, during his Red Sox career.

Stange, who toiled most of his 10 big-league seasons on the mound at Fenway Park, joined Boston on June 2, 1966, in a trade with Cleveland. During the 1967 "Impossible Dream," Stange led the staff with a 2.77 earned run average, was second in innings pitched and compiled an 8-10 record. In 1968, he anchored the bullpen with 12 saves and a 5-5 record. His totals in Boston were 28-35 with 18 rescues en route to a 62-61 career mark with 21 saves. Until the Red Sox sold the right-hander to the Chicago White Sox on June 29, 1970, Stange remained a dependable performer for Boston.

Born in Chicago on October 27, 1936, Stange signed out of college with the old Washington Senators and broke into the majors with the Minnesota Twins in 1961. He was later dealt to Cleveland and on September 2, 1964, against Washington, Stinger tied one of baseball's more *peculiar records when he struck out four men in the seventh inning. After finishing his career with the Hose of his native city, Stange returned to Boston as the team's pitching coach. Today, he works as a roving minor league instructor for the Red Sox, offering advice to young prospects.*

◆   ◆   ◆

My brother and I did something the kids today hardly ever do. It seems all we ever did growing up was play games with our friends in the neighborhood. We played baseball from sunup to sundown. When it was the football season, we played football.

At Proviso Township High, which was just outside of Chicago, Ray Nitschke and I played football and baseball together. Nitschke was a hard thrower. He had trouble finding home plate, but if you put a pigskin in his hands he could throw it the length of a football field.

Drake University recruited me to play football. In fact, the only sport I didn't play in college was baseball. I tried to play basketball but in our second scrimmage, I cut for a pass and my knee went out. That injury wiped out any chances of me playing baseball that spring.

During the summer, I had a chance to play baseball for the Drake coach who managed a semi-pro team in Estherville, Iowa. It was mostly college kids. I was released during the year but it wasn't the first time something like that happened. Some years before, someone cut another pretty good ballplayer named Moose Skowron.

I always wanted to play baseball. My size was against me for basketball and football. When I graduated high school, Otto Bluege, a scout for the Senators, said that if I ever wanted to sign a contract, let him know, which I eventually did.

The next summer, I had appendicitis and missed most of the year. I wanted to enlist in the service but Uncle Sam refused me because of my knee. So I decided to try pro baseball. I was 20 years old. I called Mr. Bluege and he sent me a contract for $200 a month to play in a Class D League. I reported to Fort Walton Beach, Florida. It was warm and humid. I recall they had mosquitoes that were big enough to carry me away.

Back then, every team had big organizations and Class D was about as low as you could go starting out. But I looked at it this way. . .the Senators had been a last place team for 20 years; if I made an impression, I'd at least get a chance to play and maybe a shot at the big leagues.

I spent two years at Fort Walton Beach. I had success my second year there, winning 13 games with a 3.36 earned-run average. The next stop was Fox Cities, Wisconsin, in the Three-I League, a B League. Compared to nowadays, B ball was more like Double A. You had some older players who had been around, at least four or five veterans with minor league experience. It was a big jump.

In those days, a pitcher could win 20 games and end up staying in the minors. There was always a message: "Go do it again. You're not ready." The feeling was you had to be 26 or 27 years old to pitch effectively in the majors. Today, a kid has two good years in the minors and he's in the big leagues. There's a totally different approach and the young kids miss a key part of development. We used to always talk baseball. If you struck out a hitter and someone else was having trouble with him, you'd talk about it. You learn baseball that way.

Fox Cities was loaded with pitchers. Four of the starters had signed big bonuses. When Calvin Griffith gave away money to someone, which didn't happen often, you knew that guy was going to pitch. It was during that year I thought about quitting but Jack McKeon, who was the manager, talked me out of it. He used me in long relief mostly. One weekend, one of the bonus kids went home to get married. I pitched in his place and threw a three-hit shutout. But as soon as he came back, I went back to the bullpen.

The next year, at Wilson of the Carolina League, McKeon gave me a regular turn. In fact, I started opening day and went on to win 20 games. I was invited to the Instructional League at St. Petersburg. The Twins had some prospects, people like Jim Kaat, Bernie Allen, Tony Oliva and Jimmie Hall. Hall was as good a centerfielder as you ever wanted to see. He could do everything. Run and hit with power. Bo Belinsky hit him in the cheekbone with a pitch later on and he was never the same hitter.

When I was called up to the Twins in 1961, they were in transition and really started to make their move the next season. Minnesota had a strong pitching staff with Camilo Pascual, Pedro Ramos, Jack Kralick and Kaat. They also had a good everyday lineup with people like Rich Rollins, Zoilo Versalles, Don Mincher, Vic Power, Earl Battey and Harmon Killebrew.

Killebrew impressed me the most. What an amazing hitter! He'd hit a ball so high, you'd swear it would never come down. One game, he hit a drive over the left field roof in Detroit. Another time, he hit one in Minnesota that was in the second deck of the bleachers. Harmon was a hard worker and that made quite an impression. He was an established player on a young team. Everyone looked up to him. You saw how hard he was working, you didn't have too many people slacking off.

What put the Twins over the hurdle was obtaining Mudcat Grant. Minnesota sent George Banks and myself to Cleveland for the Mudcat. I left a team loaded with pitching for another team that had one of the best staffs around–Sam McDowell, Luis Tiant, Sonny Siebert, Dick Donovan and Tommy John. I wasn't worried about starting there...my biggest worry was just making the team.

Despite great pitching, we did not finish high in the standings. Our defense was not exceptional, but we did have some characters like Leon Wagner. Daddy Wags played left field. Daddy Wags had trouble catching the ball but could hit home runs. He always had something new in fashion wear. He was the forerunner of Hawk Harrelson who came to Boston with the Nehru suits.

I spent two seasons in Cleveland before Don McMahon and I moved to the Red Sox in a trade for Dick Radatz. That season was rather unusual. Between the beginning and the June 15th trading deadline, the Red Sox traded 15 of the 25 guys they broke camp with. We posted the second best record in the second half but still ended up near the bottom.

That "Impossible Dream" year was really a carry-over from the second half of 1966. Dick Williams did a great job managing but we did have a pretty good ballclub. Williams is not the easiest man to play for, but baseball and strategy-wise he knew what to do.

I pitched better that year than any other season I spent in the majors. I finished 8-and-10 for a losing record but it was just a case of when it was a 2-2 game for seven innings, I'd be taken out for a pinch-hitter. The next inning, we'd score four runs.

I don't think any ballplayer that I saw ever had a bigger year than Carl Yastrzemski did in '67. Not only stat-wise but also in the field. The ball always seemed to be hit to left field and Yaz would make a helluva catch. If the tying run was on second base, he'd throw the runner out at home. Every chance we had to win a game, Yaz did it.

Five teams had a chance to win the pennant and it wasn't until the last weekend that we clinched. Jim Kaat had us shut out for four innings on Saturday. He hurt his arm and we pounded their relief pitching. Jim Lonborg pitched on Sunday and he started the big rally. We were down 2-0 and he dropped a bunt in the fifth that got us going.

Lonborg reminded me some of Sam McDowell because they could both overpower hitters. Jim threw hard and had a good breaking ball. Up until that season, he had trouble throwing strikes. In the World Series, he pitched two complete games against St. Louis and hardly gave up any hits. It was like bringing in a major league pitcher to face a high school team. That's exactly what it was like in the seventh game too, when Gibson pitched against us. Total domination.

I believe I was very fortunate during my career. I had to prove myself every year in spring training just to make the club. Minnesota wanted to make me a reliever because they said I was too small to be a starter. That was even after I won 20 games in 1960. When I went to the

Instructional League, the farm directors were convinced I could be a short reliever. What a manager liked about me was that I could come into a game and usually throw strikes. I could throw my slider for a strike. That made the manager feel somewhat confident that, at least, I could get the ball over and we had a chance to get someone out.

The biggest thing you can do to help a player is be positive. A pitcher is as good as his confidence. Pitchers tend to give the hitter too much credit. They have this attitude that if they throw a fastball over the plate, they will serve up a home run. The fastball is still an effective pitch. Instead of going after the hitter, they try to trick him. That's one thing I learned from Joe Haynes who was a vice-president with the Twins. He was a former pitcher and we'd talk about setting up the hitters.

As much as Griffith talked about his problems in Minnesota, I think he liked it out there. He had a good drawing card and always made it easy for his players. In fact, the Twins were one of the first clubs to have charter flights. But ironing out a contract was another matter. If you went to talk with Calvin one-on-one, he'd always try to compromise, not negotiate with you.

In 1963, I earned $9,000 and had a pretty good year. I had a 12-5 record and a 2.62 ERA. I went to see Calvin about a raise. I was looking for $15,000 and he almost fell off his chair.

"That's almost $1,500 a win," he said.

We settled for a little more than $1,000 a win but I guess it was a little too much for Calvin. In June, he traded me.

24

Gary Waslewski

*O*n July 6, 1969, as a member of the Montreal Expos, Gary Waslewski had his best day as a pitcher, missing a perfect game against the Philadelphia Phillies by one hit. The effort, however, hardly matched what the right-hander is best remembered for as a member of the Boston Red Sox—five strong innings in Game 6 of the 1967 World Series which helped extend the Annual Classic to a winner-take-all seventh game against the St. Louis Cardinals.

Born July 21, 1941, in Meriden, Connecticut, a city of 58,000 which is known internationally for its high-quality silver products, Waslewski spent eight years milling a craft in the minors before joining the Red Sox to be part of the "Impossible Dream." In two seasons in Boston, Waslewski compiled a 6-9 record in 36 appearances.

Overall, Waslewski spent six seasons in the majors, logging innings for St. Louis, the New York Yankees and Oakland A's. Though he posted an 11-26 overall mark and a 3.44 earned run average in 152 appearances, *he still won a place in the hearts of trivia buffs as the first pitcher to lose a major league game outside of the United States.*

◆   ◆   ◆

I was property of the Pittsburgh Pirates until the Red Sox drafted me in 1964. The following spring, I had the Triple A team in Toronto made, except that Boston was overloaded with pitchers. A number of guys were coming off good years and it was a case of the numbers. So to send me to Pittsfield–their Double A club in the Eastern League–the Red Sox had to first offer me back to Pittsburgh. Luckily, the Pirates said, "We don't want him," or my career might have ended right there.

Eddie Popowski managed the club and we had people like George Scott and Reggie Smith on the way up. "Pop" used me as a starter but also coming out of the bullpen. I got off to a good start and moved up to Triple A in about six weeks.

At the time, Toronto was not playing too well for Dick Williams. In my first appearance, I gave up five runs and retired only one batter yet made headlines the next day: **Waslewski's ERA 135.00.** So much for this phenom from Double A. I pitched in relief in a 20-0 rout and got hammered in a big inning.

Back then, the philosophy was a guy who finished what he started was a good pitcher. If you won 20 games and finished 16 games, you were pretty good. If you won 25 and had only six complete games, you weren't too good. The old macho stuff: "He can't go nine. He won't stick his head through the wall. He won't get hit by a pitch to start a rally."

Williams had his own philosophy. "Just go as long as you can. Give me six or seven innings, and we'll get someone to finish for you." And we had a guy coming out of the bullpen who made it easy for us. "Fireball" Freddie Wenz could throw pretty hard.

In today's baseball, that seems to be the trend. Teams develop a stopper for the bullpen. The Red Sox groomed Sparky Lyle for that closer role but Dick Radatz may have been Boston's first specialty pitcher. For the most part, if you were a reliever, you were somebody who couldn't make it as a starter.

The years I spent in Toronto, we won the Governor's Cup each season. We finished third in '65 but we beat everybody in the playoffs. In '66, Reggie Smith, Joe Foy, Mike Andrews and myself won big-league contracts. In early May, we were rained out of a game in Rochester so we did what teams usually do when there is a rainout. At the hotel bar, Williams got pretty snockered-down and announces, "Any of you that do a good job and win the Cup this year for me, I'll take you to Boston. The Red Sox have promised me the job if I bring home a winner." The way the parent club was playing, Billy Herman wasn't coming back and the Red Sox were looking for a new manager. Well, we won the championship again and Williams kept his word.

I've played for a few managers but not too many know their baseball like Williams. He was sharp enough so the other guys couldn't pull any tricks on you. In spring training, he went back to basics. We practiced fielding bunts until we couldn't walk. He used to love to stand up there with a fungo bat in his hands and hit rockets off your kneecap. "Catch the ball." Crack. Crack. Crack. Williams was a hard charger but he knew the game.

That spring, I had a tired arm because of playing a double season and began the year in Toronto. I threw over 200 innings and then played winter ball in Puerto Rico. By the time spring training rolled around, I had developed some tendinitis and couldn't lift my arm.

When I did get the call to Boston, I replaced Billy Rohr, the lefty who started out with that one-hitter against the Yankees. Rohr got called into the service and the Red Sox needed a pitcher. I was 26 years old and I guess it was the average age a pitcher got to the big leagues. It was an age that they figured you had pitched enough at each level and developed some type of consistency. Is he a winner? A loser? A .500 pitcher? What can we use him for?

In my first game, I pitched against the only guy who ever scared me in baseball. Frank Howard was 6-foot-7, 290 pounds and there was really no place to throw the ball over the plate because his bat was so big. Inside the batter's box, Howard could still get good wood on a ball a foot off the plate. In his second or third time up, I sawed him off so bad, Howard didn't hit the ball out of the infield—but he wound up with a hit. When he swung, I ducked and Foy ran backwards. By the time Joe picked up the dribbler down the third base line, Howard had reached first.

The thing I remember most about the "Impossible Dream" season was, I don't think anyone believed we were really going to win. We surprised a lot of people too, thinking they were playing last year's walkovers. We just went along our merry old way and kept beating people. It got contagious and everyone chipped in. A good example is when Rico Petrocelli got hurt. Jerry Adair, our utilityman, filled in for a month and played like an All-Star. If there was pressure on anyone, though, it was on Yaz. The whole game-plan was to get men on base for him. If we were behind, our strategy was to get into a position to have Yaz win it for us with a hit.

No matter when you walk out to the mound, you're nervous. Your legs always shake a little but, truthfully, I tried to look at Game 6 of the '67 World Series as just another game. There were stories in the newspapers comparing my chances with General Custer's but I didn't let it bother me. I had pitched in "must" games before and if I had my stuff, I figured I could win.

Around the sixth inning, I ran out of gas. My legs were tired and I couldn't get that second wind to continue. After I walked Roger Maris and Tim McCarver, I was losing my concentration. When Williams came out, he asked, "What do you think?" I leveled with the guy. We had a 4-2 lead and it wasn't the right time to serve up a home run. We found that out the next day when Jim Lonborg stayed out there one batter too long.

I lasted one more year in Boston and then was dealt to St. Louis for Dick Schofield. Leaving the Red Sox, at first, was devastating. But the more I started to think about it, the trade wasn't too bad after all. The Cardinals were a great team in the National League and had won back-to-back pennants. They were a classy organization and the players made you feel at home. At spring training, Dal Maxvill and McCarver welcomed me like I had been there for years.

The Cardinals had plenty of pitching, particularly Bob Gibson and Steve Carlton. At the time, Gibson was the master and Carlton was the wet-nosed kid. It was like father and son out there. Gibson had just incredible control and great stuff for nine innings. On a close pitch, he got the call. With Gibson, it was strike one, strike two and strike three on a pitch four inches off the plate.

I didn't get to pitch that long with the Cardinals but long enough, believe it or not, to lose the first major league baseball game played outside of the United States. We opened the season in Montreal in '69 and the Expos scored seven quick runs off Nelson Briles. I came on in the second inning. We eventually tied the game but in the seventh, Coco Laboy hit a double and Dan McGinn, the opposing pitcher, singled through the left side to score what proved to be the game-winner.

St. Louis was shopping for bullpen help. When the Expos made Mudcat Grant available, I was shipped to Montreal. I looked at the deal as a chance to get back into a starting rotation. At the time, the Expos were trying just about anybody. When I joined the team, Montreal had lost 18 games in a row and that didn't include a loss to their Triple A club. It was frustrating. Gene Mauch tried everything to get us out of the slump. One night, he picked the lineup out of a hat. Another time, "If I catch anyone in their room tonight, there will be a fine!" Nothing worked. The streak reached 20 before we finally beat the Dodgers.

On an expansion team, it's tough to show any consistency. Young players make young-player mistakes. A fly ball that would normally be caught drops for a hit. Grounders that are normally outs turn into errors. I once saw Mack Jones make the last out of a game because he picked up a live ball. The umpire called strike two and the ball popped out of the catcher's glove, so Mack picked up the ball and handed it to the catcher. There was a man on base so the umpire called him out. We were losing games on things like that.

I pitched in relief but in my first start for Montreal, I threw a one-hitter against the Phillies and faced the minimum 27 men. Ricardo Joseph got the only hit, a ground ball single to center in the sixth inning that just got by Bobby Wine. But we were able to turn a double play.

I finished my career with a pretty good team in Oakland. The A's were young and would have been around for a long time if Charlie Finley had kept them together. Playing for Finley was an experience. He'd fine you $25 for throwing a foul ball to a fan. Every time you turned around, there was a new face in the clubhouse. You'd have to check twice to see if your bags were packed.

Bert Campaneris was the catalyst for that team. If he got on, all hell would break loose. On the mound, a pitcher would have to make good pitches to the next batter, a guy named Joe Rudi. Next came Sal Bando, Reggie Jackson, Mike Epstein, Gene Tenace and right down the line.

Besides the hitting, Oakland had plenty of pitching. Catfish Hunter, Ken Holtzman and Vida Blue were the starters with Darold Knowles, Bob Locker and Rollie Fingers in relief. It was one reason why I played in Triple A in '73 and the rest of the American League had trouble beating the A's.

25

Joe
Lahoud

*B*orn on April 14, 1947, in a Connecticut city once known for its
fine Stetsons, Danbury's Joe Lahoud went on to wear hats of
several major league teams including the Boston Red Sox.

In 1968, Lahoud was only 21 years old when he jumped
from Class A ball to be Boston's Opening Day right fielder. Primarily a
spare outfielder, Lahoud showed power when he connected. He appeared
in 254 games over four seasons with Boston, batting just .205 but launch-
ing 26 homers among 123 hits. He had a couple of memorable games,
particularly in 1969. On June 11, Lahoud hit three home runs in a 13-5
victory at Minnesota. Against the Seattle Pilots on July 27, he homered
with a man on to win a 20-inning marathon.

Lahoud's career spanned 791 games over 11 years, including stints
with the Milwaukee Brewers, California Angels, Texas Rangers and
Kansas City Royals. He batted .223 with 65 lifetime homers. His most productive year was 1974 with the Angels, batting .271 with 13 homers and
44 RBIs in 107 games.

◆ FENWAY VOICES

Twice in his career, Lahoud was involved in multi-player deals: from Boston to Milwaukee in a 10-player deal on October 11, 1971, and then from the Brewers to California on October 22, 1973, which also had eight others exchanging uniforms.

◆   ◆   ◆

Everyone doesn't come out of baseball wealthy like a lot of people think. I had to sweat out every spring and every June 15th trading deadline. I wasn't the ballplayer who had the multi-year contract. A lot of guys can't live without baseball. For a couple of years, I almost couldn't.

The worst thing about my 14 years in the game is that the time went by like a snap of the finger. As a player, you look forward to October only if your team is out of the pennant race. A week or so after the World Series, you can't wait for spring training to begin.

I recently played in an Old-Timers Game in Boston and it was great. You're saying to yourself, "Boy, I can still play," yet when I had to run for a fly ball, my mind wanted to go but my body said no. You realize quickly that you can't bring back youth.

What I miss the most about baseball is the camaraderie in the clubhouse. You live with these guys for nine months of the year. You're constantly with these people. You may not be in the same room all the time, but for eight hours a day, you're in the buses, on the field, at the airport with them. It's like being in a huge fraternity. You could do things in a fraternity you couldn't do in school. Everyone went to class and the fraternity went out at night.

Just being around the guys that weekend brought back memories. It just so happened that the Red Sox were playing Kansas City. It must have been about 2:30 in the morning and myself, Dick Radatz and Gary Bell, were in the hotel lobby talking. Out of the corner of my eye, on the other side of the lobby, I see George Brett at the check-in desk. Day after day, hit after hit, Brett and Rod Carew were the best hitters I ever saw while I was in the big leagues. Others may have had similar physical attributes but Brett and Carew were blessed with a very special mental approach.

Brett had lost his computerized room key so he's asking the clerks to get a new one made up for him. It's kind of funny. "Mullethead" is trying to prove to the people at the desk that he's George Brett. The clerks don't believe him and George starts to raise his voice. All of a sudden, he turns around and yells, "Lahoud! I can't believe it." He proceeds to run across the lobby. He throws a body-block on me and the two of us are rolling on the floor laughing. This is George Brett, million-dollar-a-year ballplayer.

We get up from the floor and Brett puts his arm around me. He asks how things are going and says, "You know. You're still my idol. Remember when you hit 11 in a row into the upper deck at Yankee Stadium? No one will match that feat as long as I live." I couldn't shine Brett's shoes as far as ability goes but little things like that are important to me.

The performance George alluded to happened in batting practice. Every day, the scrubbies would play the regulars in a little game. Whoever hit the most home runs didn't have to buy the post-game beers. Well, I guess I just put on a show that day. In 14 swings, I hit 11 into the upper deck in right field, the same ballpark my childhood heroes played in. I grew up in southern Connecticut and would have given anything to play for the Yankees. Mickey Mantle was my idol and still is. When I got to the majors, Mantle was a coach. I wanted to show him I could hit. I wanted to show Mickey I could play.

I forget the year but we're playing the Yankees and a little ruckus starts in the infield. When something like that happens, you always grab the guy nearest to you. I found myself next to Carl Yastrzemski and Yaz was near first base where he's got Joe Pepitone in a headlock. "Pepi" wears a toupee but you'd never know it by all the hair he has. Yaz is working him over pretty good and all I can hear is Pepitone saying, "Hit my face. Hit anything but don't take my hat off. Don't upset my moss." I had more laughs with Yaz, a superstar, but also a very shy individual. Yaz was not a big guy, but pound for pound, he could generate bat speed. If you get the head of the bat on the ball, you're going to hit. During my years with the Red Sox, especially in spring training in '68, the writers were always making comparisons between the two of us. We both played the outfield. We both hit left-handed. Our swings were virtually identical. In fact, one of the Boston papers ran our pictures in the centerfold, asking "Who's Yaz?" The only difference was Yaz hit home runs to win games. I hit mine to win beers in batting practice.

I was fortunate, though, I had an attribute that the Red Sox were looking for. I could hit the ball out of the ballpark and did it with some consistency. It was one of the reasons I had gotten invited to the big league camp. Boston was also looking for an outfielder to replace Tony Conigliaro who was beaned by Jack Hamilton in '67. His misfortune, however, did not have a bearing on me coming north with the team. I hit something like .490 in spring training with a few home runs. If Joe Doe hit the way I did, any manager, including Dick Williams, would have been forced to bring him to Boston.

Because of what I did that spring, I think I earned a chance to play in the big leagues. I also got a million dollars worth of publicity, especially with the comparisons to Yaz. I was going to be the next Ted Williams.

I was going to fill Tony C's shoes. The hype was something Dick Williams had trouble accepting. Looking back at it now, I can accept what took place between myself and Williams. Winning the pennant and all, there was an ego trip somewhere in there. To see someone else getting attention, it was hard for him to take. And becoming friends with Yaz just magnified things.

I only played in 29 games in Boston that season but I started in right field Opening Day. I recall being nervous. The first ball hit to me was off the bat of Al Kaline. It was a routine play but I remember thinking the ball was never going to come down. I heard each voice among 54,220 at Tiger Stadium.

I spent all of 1969 in Boston and hit three home runs in a game in Minnesota. Ironically, I didn't play the next three weeks. Check the books. Tony Conigliaro had a neck ailment. The Red Sox took him to specialists to find out what was wrong. We had an off day and returned home for a series against Oakland. Tony C. was back in the lineup and Larry Claflin, one of the premier newspaper columnists in Boston at the time, wrote an article about it. He started by saying, "Lahoud isn't only the strongboy from Connecticut who hits home runs, but he did in one day what the doctors couldn't do for two weeks—get Tony Conigliaro back in the lineup."

It was tough to find regular work with Yaz, Hawk Harrelson, Reggie Smith, Jose Tartabull and the two Conigliaros, Tony and Billy, in the outfield. Over the winter, I asked the Red Sox for a trade so I could get a chance to play every day. Sitting on the bench in '68 and '69, I was getting staler and staler and could see what was happening to myself. If I wasn't playing when I was 21 or 22 years old, where was I going? I didn't go anywhere but, back then, where was I going to go?

At the end of spring training, the Red Sox gave me a $5,000 bonus check to report to Triple A. I didn't want the money. I wanted to play baseball and get a chance to play regularly. Throughout my career, when I got the opportunity to do that, I could hit.

In Louisville, I happened to play for Billy Gardner. "Slick" is one of the greatest guys you'd ever want to meet. In preparation for our first series, Slick has a team meeting. He goes over what's expected from the players and talks about everything, from signs to curfew. After the meeting, he called me into his office and says, "The rules I said out there are for everyone but you. You're not going to have a curfew. You're going to have a single room on the road. You do what you want to do because on this club, there are only two people who have a chance to make the big leagues. You're one of them but it's up to you. You want to blow it and stay down here for the rest of your life, go ahead. In my mind, you're capable of playing up there." The way Slick presented it to me, he made me realize I was young only once. If I was going to make it, the only person who could do something about it was me.

I went out and had one of the best years in professional baseball on a last place ballclub. With about a month left in the season, I was batting around .349 but got into a rut. My average dropped about 30 points. I was fighting myself at the plate. When you're in a slump, you try everything. I did but nothing worked.

After a night game, I came back to the hotel. Slick called me on the phone and asked what I was going to do. We had a doubleheader the next day and I told him I was going to go to sleep. "No you're not," he said. "Get your butt down to my room."

I walk down the hall to his room. There were about four others already there and what followed was an all night card game. We started about 10:30 and didn't stop until about 10:30 the next morning. Without any sleep, I went 9-for-11 in the doubleheader. Later in the clubhouse, Gardner looked at me and just laughed. "Once in a while," he said, "you just have to do that."

The Red Sox were grooming myself and Billy Conigliaro to be the next right fielder. Off the field, the two of us had our share of fist-fights but on the field, we were battling to play every day. Some time in March, around St. Patrick's Day, booze got us both traded. Eddie Kasko and Dick O'Connell were enjoying green beer and eating green spaghetti with Frank Lane, the old horse trader. The Sox were breaking up what was left of the '67 "Impossible Dream" team. They were hot after Tommy Harper. This is a good six months before the deal went down but a reporter, who was there at the time, told me this story. The more they ate and drank, the more they shuffled names back and forth. Lane wanted Jim Lonborg, Ken Brett, George Scott and Billy Conigliaro and was offering Harper, Marty Pattin and Lew Krausse. O'Connell added Don Pavletich and Lane tossed in Pat Skrable. Lane then said, "Throw in Lahoud and we got a deal." Six months later, the 10-player trade was announced.

Playing for a number of teams, you get to see plenty of players. Pitching-wise, I made a lot of pitchers look good. The ones I gave trouble to, it seemed, were sent down to the minor leagues the next day. Two of the best pitchers I ever hit against were Jim Palmer and Luis Tiant when he was with Cleveland. Palmer had such an easy motion, it looked like he was throwing harder than he actually was. He'd throw you a rising fastball or one that wouldn't rise. Then he'd cut one or slip in a real slow curve. Tiant had the finesse to go with his fastball. When Tiant was right, he could throw with anybody.

Believe me when I tell you, Nolan Ryan threw harder than anyone I ever saw. Just a class individual. I played in two of his no-hitters. I also batted against him. His biggest attribute is that he's just a bit wild. You were scared somewhat because you didn't know where Nolan's fastball was going to go.

One year, in the same game, Ryan hit me in the butt twice. Talk about accuracy. He hit me the first time and it hurt like hell. I'm going down to first base and Ryan just looks at me.

"It doesn't hurt. My daddy hit me harder than that," I said.

The next time up, Ryan hits me in the same spot. I'm doing everything in my power just to stand up. I do a slow walk to first base and I look towards the mound. Ryan is smiling behind his glove.

"Bet your daddy didn't hit you harder than that," he said.

26

Sparky Lyle

*R*eliever-supreme and the wordsmith who penned the best-selling book The Bronx Zoo, Albert "Sparky" Lyle was known for his clubhouse pranks—particularly customizing a birthday cake with a quick drop of his pants. But on the mound, especially with the game on the line, Lyle was all business.

From 1967 to 1982, the southpaw with a hard slider racked up 222 saves, a 99-76 record and established several American League records including most games without a start (807), most innings as a relief pitcher (1,265), most games finished (599) and the first reliever to win the Cy Young Award.

Born July 22, 1944, in Dubois, Pennsylvania, Lyle gained the attention of scouts in 1963 when he struck out 31 men in a 17-inning sandlot game. Signed by the Baltimore Orioles, Lyle was eventually secured in the minor league draft by the Boston Red Sox.

In four years with the Bosox, Lyle appeared in 260 games, posted a 22-19 record and saved 69 games before being dealt to the New York

Yankees on March 22, 1972, for first baseman Danny Cater and shortstop Mario Guerrero. To a degree, the event reminded Red Sox fans of the Babe Ruth transaction five decades earlier. Although Lyle was not the dominant player that Ruth was, he did become the game's premier bullpen specialist.

In his first year in the Bronx, Lyle wound up recording 35 saves, posting a 1.92 earned run average and winning the American League's Fireman of the Year honors. In 1976, Lyle also led the circuit in saves with 23 and in 1977, he captured the Cy Young Award. Lyle rolled up outstanding numbers—a league-high 72 appearances, a 13-5 record, 26 saves and 2.17 ERA—to help the Yankees to the World Championship.

Lyle spent another season in New York but had fewer save opportunities since Rich Gossage, signed as a free agent, took over as the bullpen ace. On November 10, 1978, the Yankees dispatched Lyle in a multiplayer swap with Texas which secured pitcher Dave Righetti from the Rangers. Before retiring after the 1982 season, Lyle also pitched for the Philadelphia Phillies and the Chicago White Sox.

◆ ◆ ◆

I accomplished a few things in the big leagues but to play 17 years, I was one of the most fortunate people on this earth. There are only 750 players in the major leagues. I don't care what country they come from. They are the best on the planet, as Bill Lee would say.

I was lucky to play baseball when I did. There is no way I can look back and say, "Gee, you should have done this or that." You just can't do it. I'm happy I got out of baseball when I did. I probably could have played a year or two more but, at least, when people remember Sparky Lyle, they are going to remember how he used to pitch.

I forget his name now but I recall a guy who was a good pitcher for the Pirates. He was hanging on late in his career and he just wasn't close to what he once was. That was one thing I didn't want.

Leaving the Red Sox is something I didn't want either. If Eddie Kasko hadn't been the manager, I might have never been traded. Eddie didn't think I was tough enough on left-handers. Back then, I didn't face that many lefties except for maybe Bobby Murcer, Boog Powell and Rod Carew—but I got them out pretty well, too. Kasko and I had our differences, and it wasn't long after that I was traded to the Yankees.

If I did have a contribution to baseball, I think I brought the reliever "out in the open," so to speak. Managers have always depended on a guy like that, but I don't think the philosophy in baseball, at the time, realized how crucial such a position would become. So maybe I come along and prove you don't need this righty-lefty stuff anymore. You need a guy who can come in and shut the other team down in the late innings to win the ballgame. All I wanted was the last out of that ballgame—when we were ahead.

When you take the mound, you have to be—and don't take this out of context—"Ready to kill" to win that game. I'm not talking about knock-down pitches and crap like that. I mean you have to place yourself in a type of shell so you block out everything and just see that catcher's glove. That's the intensity level you have to have to do your job. You have to come into a game and throw strikes. Any time a reliever gets in trouble, it's either on a 2-2 pitch or a full count. I could throw five innings and throw 50 or 60 pitches but now, everyone wants to see the strikeout. Still, the bottom line is to win. They don't really give a damn how you do it.

That's why the teams I played on in New York were so good. We had mental toughness, whatever it took to get mad or get where you're supposed to be to have that intensity. No one can tell you how to do it. We just had a great conglomeration of talent and players. Some thought we were washed up or shouldn't have been there but every guy contributed in his own little way.

Ralph Houk was the type of guy who treated everyone like a man. The players loved playing for him. He was quite a legend himself, you know. You called him "Major" because of the incredible things he did in World War II. The atmosphere around the clubhouse and the winning was projected through Houk. A player has to give a little extra and that comes from the player himself. Either you have it inside you or you don't, but Ralph would find a way to make sure you gave it your best.

The same goes for Billy Martin. One of the best teams I ever played on was in '76, regardless of us getting swept in the World Series. We were a pennant contender and that was a good educational experience. That was the first time for many of us to go through the playoffs and a World Series. When you win a game like we did when Chris Chambliss hit that home run in the playoffs against the Royals, it really drains you. I could never say we could have beaten Cincinnati but I'll put it this way. . . it would have been a better series if we didn't come off an emotional series like we did against Kansas City. The Big Red Machine was an awesome team, but you could pitch to them very easily. It was one of those things. We weren't mentally tough enough, at the time, to endure the playoffs and World Series. In '77, we had basically the same club. We were prepared for what we had to do. It was really something special to see and be a part of.

Thurman Munson was one of the greatest players I ever had the fortune of knowing. He was mentally and physically tough. We became good friends because, when I first joined the Yankees, he said, "What do you want from me when you come into a game?" I said, " I want you to put your groin on top of that slider if I throw it in the dirt." I could not throw one by the man. He was our leader, not from his mouth, but by doing things. Thurman touched everybody. It was a tragic thing that happened but as the players knew, if he was going to leave life early, that's how Thurman was going to go—in an airplane. Flying was his hobby.

I was always a very intense player, no matter what sport I played. One reason was because I loved defense. I was never that much of an offensive-type person. I scored touchdowns and points in basketball but the defensive part of the game is where I excelled. If you are defensive-oriented, you're going to be a little tougher than an offensive-minded guy. As a relief pitcher, you are the most important defensive man on the ballclub.

I always wanted to be a relief pitcher. I looked at it the same way as working for my dad. He was a carpenter and I used to help him. I hit my thumb a few times until I learned how to hit a nail correctly, too. Baseball is the same thing. The minors are filled with those "diamonds in the rough." You get plenty of instruction but you have to pick out what applies to you. I saw guys not make it, not because they didn't have the ability, but because they tried to apply everything they heard.

One spring with the Red Sox, I pitched against Florida State in an exhibition. I struck out maybe 12 or 14 collegians. After the game, I was feeling pretty good in the clubhouse but the next thing I heard was this tremendous voice waking me up pretty quick.

"Where's that bush left-hander who pitched today?"

The speaker was Ted Williams, the greatest hitter who ever lived, the man who turned me into a pitcher. Williams said I didn't throw hard enough to make the big leagues and there was no way I was going to fool big-league hitters with my thumb sticking up and giving away my curveball. He thought I had potential as a pitcher but the only way I'd have a chance to reach the bigs was to develop a slider. Williams said it was the only pitch that he couldn't consistently hit, even when he knew it was coming! And Williams had that knack to know which pitches they'd throw his way.

Williams never showed me how to throw the slider but he told me how the pitch was supposed to break. I used to lie awake in bed at night, trying to figure out how to get the ball to break like he said. Most people throw a slider by turning their hand with a three-quarter flick of the wrist. I threw over the top and it gave me a more devastating slider. Instead of the pitch breaking in towards a hitter and then going down, mine would come in and go straight down. As long as the ball is going down, if the hitter does make contact, you'll get the ground ball. It became my strike pitch and the amazing thing is I didn't need to have good location.

Eddie Popowski helped me a great deal, too, because he'd get on my case. "Pop" always felt my concentration wasn't what it should have been when I was pitching. He'd see me have a really good showing but I'd make one bad pitch and it would cost us a ballgame. He instilled in me the fact that if I was going to be a relief pitcher, there is no room for error. "Pop" would go by and say, "Hey, Lyle. You can't be doing that out there. You want to play this job, you can't make mistakes. We're in the eighth or ninth inning here, not in the first or second inning."

I can remember going into a game with the bases loaded, giving up three runs, getting no one out and leaving with the bases loaded, too. The thing was, I was learning. Maybe I laughed about it or whatever, but I laughed about my wins, too. I just wasn't the type of guy who would go in and tear up a clubhouse. If that's what a team wanted, they hired Lou Piniella.

I was always known as "Sparky." My father called me that and it stuck. In high school, one teacher called me "Albert" and I never answered back. Maybe that's why I flunked that course.

I grew up in Reynoldsville, Pennsylvania, a town of about 2,300 people. I think there are still 2,300 people there today. Heck, there were only 90 kids in my graduating class and that was one of the largest ever to come out of Reynoldsville High. I played football and basketball because the school did not have a baseball program.

I never did have a chance to play organized ball until I was 17 years old. Whatever the season was, though, I was always playing sports. I'd come home from school, change my clothes and head to the ball field. My mother and father never gave me a set time to be home for supper because they knew where I would be. I played against kids a year or so older and I think that helped me. I had to figure out how to beat them a different way since they were bigger and physically stronger.

My personality comes from my grandmother who is at least 90 now. I can remember my father raising his voice, you know, the way you have to sometimes talk to older people who are hard of hearing.

"DON'T DO THIS. DON'T DO THAT," my father would say.

My grandmother would just sit there and nod.

When my dad left the room, she'd turn to me and say, "the older you get, the more they holler."

My grandmother never got mad at anybody. I try to live that way. You can get yourself out of most situations being a nice guy instead of telling someone to "Go scratch." I always felt you really have to work at being an SOB. There is no reason to be in a bad mood after a good night's sleep, yet some people get up that way.

Damned if I know.

27

Eddie
Kasko

*E*ddie Kasko's life in baseball has taken him from the playing
field to the manager's office to the position of Director of Scouting for the Boston Red Sox.

Born June 27, 1931, Kasko broke into professional baseball
in 1949 with Baltimore of the International League. After six minor
league seasons, interrupted by military commitments, Kasko started in the
majors in 1957 with the St. Louis Cardinals and concluded with the Red
Sox in 1966. Over the 1,077-game stretch, Kasko posted a .264 lifetime
batting average and was a capable gloveman at either second base, shortstop or third base.

Kasko spent two years in St. Louis before moving to Cincinnati in a
trade. With the Reds, Kasko emerged as an everyday contributor. He
batted a career-high .292 in 1960 and then anchored the infield at shortstop for the pennant winners in 1961. In the World Series against the New
York Yankees, Kasko batted .318.

Dealt to Houston in 1964, Kasko was named the Astros' first team *captain. Just before the start of the 1966 season, Kasko landed in Boston in a trade for second baseman Felix Mantilla. Injuries limited his effectiveness but Kasko managed to appear in 58 games. That fall, the Red Sox hired Kasko to pilot their Triple A affiliate in the International League.*

When Boston dismissed Dick Williams in 1970, Kasko was hired and he stayed at the helm through 1973. During his tenure, the Bosox placed second twice and third twice. In 1972, the Red Hose missed the American League East Division title by a half-game.

◆　　　◆　　　◆

I grew up in Linden, New Jersey. My parents owned a small neighborhood grocery store. My mother and father knew nothing about baseball. They were from the old school that, you know, if you're not going to make a living at it, why do it.

I did my chores around the store to help my folks but I always found time to play baseball. A number of major league teams held tryout camps throughout New Jersey and every year I went to as many as I could.

Frank Burke of the New York Giants ran the session one year in Perth Amboy and looking back at it now, Frank must have been one helluva scout. All he had us do was take three swings, run a 60-yard dash, and field about a dozen ground balls. I think I had number 363 or something.

After the tryout, I was one of six to get invited to spring training by the Giants. I got a contract for $150 a month. Since I was only 17 years old, I needed my father to co-sign it.

I rushed home and told my father I needed his signature on my contract.

"What for?" he said.

"To play baseball," I said.

"What do you mean?"

"I'm going to get $150 a month."

"What the hell for? Nobody is going to pay you to play baseball. They can use the parking lot and play for nothing."

I explained it again and my father finally understood. We argued a little more but he agreed to sign the contract.

The Giants sent me everything I needed to go to spring training in 1948, including a round-trip bus ticket from New York City to Sanford, Florida. I was so excited about going to play baseball, it wasn't until we got to the Carolinas that I realized the New York Giants trained in Arizona. When I arrived, I turned in the other half of the bus ticket and was assigned to work out with a Class D club in the Florida State League which, at the time, was based in Sanford.

The first day of spring training, everyone went out to a position. I was a shortstop. I looked around and there were about nine other shortstops. I was wondering what these guys were doing in my position. I had signed a contract with the Giants and I felt like that was the answer to it all. I figured the other fellows were just trying out.

About a week goes by, and I was out there with six others. A day or so later, there were five of us.

I said to one of the guys, an older fellow, "Where's Joe and where's Harry?"

"They've been released," he said.

"Released?"

"Yeah. Don't you read the blackboard in the morning when you come down for breakfast?"

"I see a bunch of names on there. I don't know what it's for."

"They get the other half of the bus ticket."

I started to wonder right then when I was going to get the other half of my bus ticket. I read that list every day and it eventually got down to two players, myself and another shortstop. I don't remember his name now but he'd been in the Florida State League for five years. He was 26 years old and was part-owner of a clothing store. He stayed and within three days, I was on my way home.

"See, I told you so," my father said. "Now make yourself useful. Go help your mother."

I pitched in around the store but I continued to go to tryout camps. In June, the Cardinals held one and they wanted to take me to spring training, a deal just like I had with the Giants. But I wasn't interested in going that route again.

I did want to play baseball, though, and a friend of mine in Linden knew Butch Voigt who had spent a little time with the Dodgers. Voigt was with Baltimore, an independently-owned ballclub in the International League. He got me a tryout when Baltimore came to play Jersey City at Roosevelt Stadium.

It's a little ironic because Tommy Thomas, who was the Baltimore general manager at the time, later scouted for the Red Sox for years and years. Throughout my career with the Red Sox, either playing or managing or scouting, Tommy always told me, "I got you where you are today. You owe me your life."

I worked out with Baltimore for three days and commuted back and forth to Linden. After the third day, Tommy came up to me and said, "We go to Newark tomorrow. If you come to Newark, your pay will start. I'll pay you $250 a month and we'll keep you with the Baltimore club for the rest of the year. Next year, we'll farm you out."

I stayed with Baltimore and played in three or four games, maybe batted nine times. It was good experience for me and the next year I went to a Class D League team and was on my way.

When I reached the big leagues with the Cardinals, we played the Dodgers at Ebbets Field. My brother got tickets for my mother and father to see me play.

"Where's Eddie playing?" my father asked.

"In Brooklyn," my brother said. "We have to start early because they're expecting 30,000 people."

"Are you crazy? That many people to see a baseball game? You're out of your mind."

My father shook his head but he went along.

That night, there was an hour rain delay before things finally started. The game went extra innings and we didn't get out of there until about 1:15 in the morning.

The next day, we played an afternoon game against the Dodgers. My parents and brother again came to see me. I forget who was pitching but it was one of those fast games. It was over in less than two hours. I was out of the clubhouse and dressed by quarter to five.

"Eddie," my father asked, "what the hell kind of a job you got? How are you going to make a living doing this? Last night, you work until 1:15. Today, you quit before 5 o'clock."

My father didn't understand the irregularities of it all, but few in his generation did. They went to work early in the morning and didn't stop until five in the afternoon.

With the Cardinals, I started out as their utilityman and wound up playing a lot at third. Ken Boyer was an all-star third baseman, but for some reason he had all kinds of problems that year in the field. Fred Hutchinson wanted to keep his bat in the lineup and was thinking of moving Kenny to the outfield, since center fielder Bobby Gene Smith, a rookie, was not hitting.

We had played about 20 games or so and Hutch came up to me one day and asked if I had ever played third base. I told him I had. "Well," he said, "you're in there today."

I had never played third in my life but if Hutchinson thought I could play there, and it was a chance to play, I was going to try it.

Well, Boyer looked like dynamite and played center field like he had been there all his life. Kenny played the rest of the year out there. He had a good arm and was a big, strong athlete.

I adjusted to playing third base. Fielding is reaction time and hand-and-eye coordination. You do a lot of the same things at third as you would at shortstop only you have less time to react. You can circle or move into a ball at short. At third, everything was sort of a jab.

One of the best things that happened to me was rooming with Sal Maglie. For some reason, they put us together and he said to me, "Look, I snore. I have trouble keeping roommates so if I keep you awake, don't feel bad about getting someone else."

"Sal," I said, "snoring doesn't bother me."

Little did I know.

Anyway, Sal was a good teacher. He's also the first one who sort of indoctrinated me to room service.

One morning I'm getting dressed and he said, "Where are you going?"

"I'm going down to breakfast?"

"Why don't we have breakfast up here?"

"Up here?"

"Yeah. What do you want to eat? Pancakes?"

"Fine."

Sal picked up the phone and the next thing I know, a waiter comes into our room wheeling in a cart with food. I had never seen anything like this before in my life.

Over breakfast, Sal starts telling me how he is going to pitch to Milwaukee. He went over each hitter, right down the lineup.

"When Wes Covington comes to bat," he said, "and you're playing shortstop, shade him a little towards the hole. Move a couple of steps towards third."

"Sal, he pulls a ball pretty good."

"Covington isn't going to get a ball to hit through the middle. If he gets anything, he's going to hit a ball in the hole."

Maglie continued going over the hitters. "When Aaron bats, play him towards the middle. When Adcock hits, shade toward the hole."

"Sal, Adcock is a dead pull hitter. Every ball he pulls, you know, I have no chance on anyway."

"Just do what I tell you."

That day, it was like I was playing shortstop in a rocking chair. Every ball Adcock hit was in the hole. Maglie could have a hitter hit a ball where he wanted it to go. That's how good a pitcher he was.

I got traded to Cincinnati and again played for Hutchinson. Hutch was a player's manager. "Just go out and play. Don't think about what you're doing." That was Hutch. He wasn't much for finesse.

Our '61 ballclub was a good group of regulars and others who sort of filled in. We were a team of misfits. Jim Brosnan was the team author. I was a guy who chewed towels. Brosnan was always reading a book or taking notes for one. I'd be on the bench pulling strings out of a towel with my teeth. It got to a point where the players would ask me, "Who has the best towels?" or "Have you tried the purple ones in Pittsburgh?"

I wouldn't see a guy I had played with for a while and he'd come across the field and throw me a towel and say, "Start chewing. You look lost without this."

We also had some players in Cincinnati who had what they now call "career" years. Gene Freese came over from Chicago and had a good year for us. So did Gordy Coleman. Our big guys were Wally Post, Gus Bell, Vada Pinson and Frank Robinson. Jerry Lynch was just an unbelievable pinch-hitter. He had 19 hits coming off the bench. For pitchers, Joey Jay, Jim O'Toole and Bob Purkey were our Big Three.

Competitive-wise, Frank Robinson was the toughest player I ever saw. He hit behind Pinson, and Frank would be in the on-deck circle calling Don Drysdale every name in the book. Drysdale would knock Pinson down and Robinson would use some more expletives, all the time knowing he's going to bat next. He was a plate-cracker and played with no fear. Frank would stand in there, maybe about six inches off the plate and almost dared you to throw at him. Pitchers would knock him down but he would get right back up and hit a home run. Frank did the little things too. If he was on first base, it didn't matter if it was a 10-1 ballgame or a 2-1 ballgame. On a ground ball, he was going to take whoever covered second into left field.

I got a chance to play with Pete Rose when he first came up to Cincinnati. By his hustling and desire, you knew that Pete was going to be good but you didn't know he was going to have the durability or become the type of player he did.

Joe Morgan was another strong, little player I was fortunate to see break in when I was moved over to Houston. You could tell Morgan was going to be durable. He worked at becoming a second baseman. In his early years, I don't think anybody visualized that he was going to have the power he had. Joe could run but what I remember about him as a hitter is that he had a quick bat.

I finished up with the Red Sox in 1966 as the utilityman but I spent more time in the hospital than playing. I could see it was close to the end of the line. After the season, I was given my release. Dick O'Connell, who was the general manager at the time, offered me a chance to stay in the organization. I managed at Toronto and then Louisville. When the Red Sox replaced Dick Williams, O'Connell offered me the job.

The only reason I took the job in Boston is because I like working for good people and Boston is one of the best organizations to work for in baseball. The years I was in the dugout, we never had the guys to run out of the bullpen. We had roughly a seven-man staff with Sonny Siebert, Ray Culp, Bill Lee, Marty Pattin, Gary Peters, John Curtis and Luis Tiant. It would have been easier for everybody if we had a couple of relievers.

Tiant was the most amazing pitcher I managed in Boston. You look back at all the guys who have had arm trouble – after one season, you don't know if they will ever come back. It is easier for a young guy to do it, but Tiant was a pitcher I believed in despite the 1-and-7 record he had when he joined us in '71. The next spring, I told Luis to work on his own schedule because he was going to be one of my pitchers. I was told we had some good, young arms in our organization but to this day, I don't remember who they were. I was sure the kids were not going to walk in here and do the job of a healthy guy who had once won 21 games. Tiant needed time and when he got himself going and regained his control, he was our best pitcher.

Darrell Johnson took over in '74 and the Red Sox kept me on as an advance scout for the big leagues. Tommy Thomas was 70 or so and Dick O'Connell was looking for a replacement.

"I just don't want you to be a regular scout," O'Connell said. "You'll be our executive scout."

"Does that mean I scout the executives?" I asked.

"Christ no. Stay away from the executives."

And I've been scouting the players ever since.

28

Tommy Harper

*T*ommy Harper played for the Red Sox in the early 1970s and brought a base-running flair which had not been seen in Boston in 60 years. In 1973, when Harper broke Tris Speaker's club record for steals, he became the sixth Red Sox in history to lead the American League in stolen bases (54).

Born October 14, 1940, in Oak Grove, Louisiana, Harper grew up in Alameda, California, and signed with the Cincinnati Reds in 1960 out of San Francisco State. When Harper reached the big leagues with the Reds, he played the outfield as well as the infield. A regular in 1965, Harper led the National League in runs scored (126). His stay in the National League ended on November 21, 1967, when the Reds struck a deal with the Cleveland Indians for first baseman Fred Whitfield and pitcher George Culver.

Harper lasted one year in Cleveland and when the American League held an expansion draft on October 15, 1968, to fill the rosters of the newly formed Seattle Pilots and Kansas City Royals, he followed Don Mincher *as Seattle's second selection in the lottery. With the Pilots, Harper batted only .235 but led the AL in stolen bases (73)—the highest total since 1915 when Ty Cobb pilfered 96. The following year, when the team moved to Milwaukee, Harper joined the "30-30 Club" by slamming 31 homers and stealing 38 bases. After another productive year, Harper was involved in a 10-player deal between the Red Sox and the Brewers on October 10, 1971, which brought the outfielder to Fenway Park. During his three years with the Red Sox, Harper batted .259 and stole 107 bases.*

Harper spent parts of 1975 with California and Oakland—appearing as a pinch-hitter in the playoffs—and finished up his career with Baltimore in 1976. Overall, he batted .257 in 1,810 games with 146 home runs and 408 steals.

Upon retiring, Harper worked in several capacities for the Red Sox. He was a coach from 1980 to 1984 and later served as a roving instructor in the minor leagues. After being dismissed by the Bosox in 1986, Harper sued the ballclub, claiming that the baseball team was racially biased in its hiring practices. The case was settled out of court and the Red Sox have since improved their minority employment opportunities. Today, Harper is a coach for the Montreal Expos.

◆　　◆　　◆

To survive in this game, you need a mental toughness. Carl Yastrzemski used to say that all the time. I don't know if fans realize it, but when you're in the big leagues, you have to play to win, not only for 162 games, but to keep your position on the ballclub. When you can last 20 years like Yaz or Henry Aaron did, you know you've done a good job.

It's tough to be a regular in the big leagues. People go into slumps and fans boo you. You are going to go 0-for-4, 0-for-8 or 0-for-12. It's only three games but when you're in a slump, the next five or six at-bats are important ones, especially with men on base. It all adds up to a lot of pressure, mentally and physically.

One year in Boston, Eddie Kasko benched me. I was hitting .100 at the time and I knew why he sat me down. In baseball, like anything else, you have to face facts. Some guys hit .071 and if the manager takes them out, they start moaning and groaning. Have you ever seen a manager bench a .300 hitter? If he does, he won't do it for a long time. Getting benched goes along with the mental toughness. You have to say, "Hey, I'm going to get my swing back and I'll be fine," and go work at it. The year Kasko did that to me was the best thing that ever happened. He gave me a chance to get out of the daily rat race and get my mind together. I was able to relax and come back fresh. I wound up being the MVP for the Red Sox that season.

Boston was a chance for me to continue playing. In baseball, you can't worry about being traded because there is nothing you can do about it. You go and do the best you can. It's no big deal. It's a way of life. They pay you to play, not to run the ballclub.

I've always found that the less you have on your mind, the better off you'll be. I learned that from Dave Bristol in the minor leagues. Bristol had a saying, "Just don't let it concern you." And he said that a lot. Pretty soon, it made plenty of sense. There are so many things you really don't have control over, so why get yourself worked up over them? I'd hear a couple of the guys talking in May, saying something like, "In September, do you know we have to go from Oakland to Minnesota?" Like I said, why worry about it?

If you are going to make it, you'll make it. Anyone can get through the maze of anything if you do the job. When I talk to kids in school, I try to tell them to think about getting an education because you have to be prepared for other things in life. Every kid wants to play professional sports but you need schooling. You can't go to school just to be a pro athlete. You have to study and be a well-rounded person. You don't think about failure but you have to be ready in life for whatever comes up. You don't fail sometimes because of ability. You might because of injury.

With me, baseball is really close to home. Growing up, I was inspired by my older brother. I knew of Jackie Robinson and his story and of Larry Doby but, quite honestly, my brother kept me involved in baseball. Syl bought me spikes and my first glove. He made sure I had the equipment to play. Syl played semi-pro ball and was a pretty good pitcher. I was maybe 12 or 13 years old and I'd tag along with Syl, just in case his team was short a player.

I played baseball because it was fun. It wasn't until my senior year in high school that I really started to think about pro baseball, because one of my Legion coaches said, "Tommy, if you concentrated on one sport, you'd have a chance to play in the majors." I played football, basketball and also ran track. So that's what I eventually did. In college, I just played baseball.

In high school, I played with Willie Stargell and Curt Motton. The three of us also were together in Legion ball, the same program that Frank Robinson played in when Oakland Post 337 won a national championship. That's when I really started thinking about baseball. Bobby Mattick, who later managed the Blue Jays, was a bird-dog scout for the Reds and he coached us. He signed Robinson, Vada Pinson and myself. In those days, there was no baseball draft. You signed if the opportunity came along.

Dave Bristol and Johnny Vander Meer were my managers in the minors and when I made it to Cincinnati, Fred Hutchinson was in charge. When I first came up, I was an outfielder. In spring training, Gene Freese broke an ankle and Hutch asked me if I could play third base. I gave it a try but it was a short experiment. I had never played third before. To learn the position, the Reds sent me to San Diego in the Coast League for seasoning. They knew my best position was in the outfield but there was no room out there with Robinson, Pinson, Wally Post, Marty Keough and Jerry Lynch. Except for a few games here and there, my last year at third base was in the minors.

Before I joined the Red Sox, I came to Milwaukee by way of Seattle. I was taken in the expansion draft from Cleveland and the Seattle franchise ended up shifting to Milwaukee. The people in Milwaukee were happy to get a team back. It wasn't the old Braves with Hank Aaron but it was baseball. The players were in the same frame of mind I was. It was an opportunity to play. If I had stayed on the bench in Cleveland, I might have been out of baseball. As it turned out, I was able to play for eight more years.

I usually stole between 20 to 28 bases a year and considered myself a decent baserunner. I only stole a base when it meant something, say early in a game, to help us get a runner in scoring position. That year in Seattle when I stole 73 bases, we just didn't have a good team. Joe Schultz was managing and he told me to run any time I wanted to. I ran on the pitcher but I also learned by observing what others did or by trying different things, maybe getting a bigger lead against a certain pitcher. Watching games on TV gives you a pretty good angle. You're not going to get picked off base sitting in your living room but you can learn by studying habits of people. When I was coaching or working with the minor leaguers, I told the young guys to watch as many games as possible to gain experience. It's like reading a book. In school, you read other people's philosophies and styles to help form your own ideas. You see something you like, take note of it. The same holds true in baseball.

29

John
Kennedy

*F*rom 1970 to 1974, Boston fans knew him as "Super Sub." On that label rests John Kennedy's recognition in baseball. No matter which team the spirited infielder played for, Kennedy could perform admirably at shortstop, second base or third base.

Born in Chicago on May 29, 1941, Kennedy signed with the Washington Senators out of high school. His 12-year stay in the majors began in 1962 in the nation's capital when a more famous man named John Kennedy was President of the United States. Following three years on teams which lost 100 or more games, Kennedy was traded to Los Angeles. He was a spare for the Dodgers, a team which made back-to-back appearances in the World Series—winning it all in 1965.

Before joining the Red Sox, Kennedy spent a year with the New York Yankees, a season with the Seattle Pilots and part of 1970 with the Milwaukee Brewers. When his contract was secured from Portland of the Pacific League, Kennedy quickly became a Hub favorite with his aggressive style. For his career, Kennedy played in 856 games and batted

.225 with 32 homers. He now works for the Commonwealth of Massachusetts in the tax department.

◆   ◆   ◆

One of the biggest compliments in my life came from a fan at a Bosox Club luncheon some years back. This woman came up to me and said, "If there were only more people like you and Johnny McKenzie, sports would be so much better." To me, that was rewarding because Johnny McKenzie, when he played hockey, went full-bore, hitting and smashing people into the boards. Johnny probably didn't have the greatest ability in the world but he just went after it 100 percent. That's the way I played and really, that's the only way to play.

I can remember the first couple of years I played in the majors. I'd pop balls up and I'd run like a maniac. I'd be screaming as hard as I was running. "You dummy. You no good son of a buck." A lot of guys would be popping it up, swearing and hollering too, but they wouldn't be running.

I have no doubt there were plenty of guys better than me who never played in the big leagues. I didn't think about who was in front of me or who I had to get by to get there. I just felt I was good enough to play and had that confidence in my ability. I played hard because I always felt that if I did that, I'd have peace of mind. I didn't want to go to my grave wondering if I could have played in the big leagues.

I managed in the minors for a few years and that's what I always told the kids who played for me. Don't go to your grave saying, "If I did this, I'd have been a millionaire. I could have been a big leaguer and my family would have been well off. I could have taken care of Mom and Dad, my wife, my kids, her family. If I only would have done this." Go to your grave knowing that you were short on ability. Give it your best shot. If it wasn't good enough, you can live with yourself.

When fans see players going out there and playing hard, sliding and diving and running, that sticks out in their minds. I don't care how good you are. If you don't show an effort out there, somewhere on that scouting report, someone is going to write down, "A dog. Doesn't hustle." That says more than numbers to an organization. When things aren't going good, the guy doesn't put out. Not recommended. When I was managing the Red Sox in Bristol, Connecticut, some of the outfielders were complaining. They said, "How am I going to play for the Red Sox?" I said, "Well, you're not." They'd back off, you know, wondering what are you talking about? I said, "You are not going to play the outfield for the Red Sox because they've got Lynn, Yastrzemski, Rice, Evans and Carbo. But if you're good enough to play in the big leagues, you'll play there." Ideally, you want to play for the organization which drafts you but the main objective for anyone is to play in the big leagues. If you're good enough to play, you'll play. Trades do come up. Scouts have to write reports on guys who are in the minors because some will be left unprotected in the draft. When names are discussed, they look at the reports. You never know. You might go to an organization that doesn't have any outfielders. A kid could be in the big leagues next year.

Remember Joe Lefebvre. He had some big years at West Haven as did some of the others in the Yankee organization. I was coaching there and the kids were talking about the same sort of thing. I can remember hearing Joe say, "I don't care who I play in the big leagues with." He had something inside that a lot of players don't. He had the driving factor, the desire. Just a hard-nosed player.

Lefebvre came out of New Hampshire and nobody wanted him. Another kid from New Hampshire was Steve Balboni. Bill Livesey, who's now with the Yankees, was coaching down at Eckert College. He called up Jack Butterfield, who since passed away, and said, "I'm telling you. I've got some kids from New England who can play." Lefebvre got a chance to play but unfortunately, he got hurt. All Balboni does is hit home runs.

Speaking of homers, I'm one of a number of players to hit one in my first at bat. Do you know it almost took me five years to hit my second?

We were playing Minnesota and Dick Stigman is pitching a no-hitter. All of sudden, Mickey Vernon wants me to pinch-hit. When he called my name, I almost died. I was scared to death. The only other big league pitcher I faced was Early Wynn but I never swung the bat. In spring training, he struck me out on three pitches. I said to myself, if I'm going to strike out, strike out swinging. The first pitch was down in the dirt and I swung at it. The next pitch was a foot inside and I hit it out. I ran around the bases in what must have been the fastest time in history. When I got to the dugout, I couldn't breathe. Vernon, to this day, says I looked white as a ghost.

There was another famous John Kennedy in Washington. I never really had the opportunity to meet the President, but there was an awful lot written about us. Our birthdays are on the same date. They said we used to exchange birthday cards which we never did. But it got into the papers one time and naturally, every town I went into, the question always came up. I would just tell them it wasn't true.

The only incident that ever happened was that my wife, Betty, who was my fiancee at the time, had written me a letter from Chicago and it went to the White House by mistake. I wound up getting this big envelope in the mail from the Office of the President. I was wondering what he was sending me. Inside the envelope was a letter from Betty.

Leaving Washington was hard at first. There was an article in the paper that the Senators were going to try to build the whole ballclub around Eddie Brinkman, Claude Osteen and myself. That winter, two of us were traded, Osteen and myself, to the Dodgers. Junior Gilliam had retired and I was handed the third-base job. But I pulled a muscle and it got so bad I couldn't play, so the Dodgers coaxed Gilliam out of retirement.

Junior ended up hitting .282 that year and was quite instrumental, along with a lot of others, in us winning the pennant. When I came back, Alston told me he couldn't sit Gilliam down and that's how that utility role came about. I'd fill in here and there. Somewhere along the line, I'd have a good series against a team, impress someone and sooner or later, they'd be looking for a reserve-type player. As it turned out, I lasted in the big leagues for a good 10 or 11 years. If I had played regularly, I could have been gone after two or three years.

Going to the Dodgers was a complete change. The situation in Washington was tough to handle and I could see how people might acquire a defeatist attitude. You'd always be saying you're going to win but on the ride to the ballpark, you'd start thinking the Yankees had Mantle, Maris, Howard, Ford and everybody else. We were no match for them. It's hard to believe, a year later, I was on a team that swept the Yankees in the World Series. The Dodgers had some outstanding names too— Koufax, Drysdale, Podres, Wills, the Davises.

Truthfully, I was nervous about going over there but I also realized that this team had a shot at doing something. We were quite fortunate to win the pennant in '65 and '66 without a very good team batting average. But if we scored two or three runs a game, we were almost assured of winning because of the outstanding pitching.

On any day Koufax took the mound, you had a feeling he could pitch a no-hitter. The last two years of his career, Sandy won 53 games. In spring training one year, his arm was bothering him so bad, they had to send him back to Los Angeles. I would describe his arm like a sausage in a casing. If you took your finger and poked his arm, you'd puncture the skin. That's how swollen his arm was. He didn't pitch much that spring but wound up winning 26 games that season.

I played in Sandy's perfect game. As a utilityman, I'd replace Gilliam in the late innings. That's all I could think about. Getting into the game in the eighth or ninth and booting a ball to goof up the whole thing. Well, Koufax struck out the last six guys and I never got a chance. The last two, Joe Amalfitano and Harvey Kuenn, never took their bats off their shoulders. That's how hard he was throwing. After the game, I congratulated Sandy and told him I was nervous. Sandy laughed. "JK," he said, "when I looked over and saw you there, I knew I didn't want anybody to hit the ball."

Baseball is something I always wanted to do. It's in my baby book. My father had written it in. President Roosevelt died when I believe I was three years old. My dad and I were playing marbles on the living room floor. He said to me, "Would you like to be President some day?" I said, "No. I want to be a ballplayer." I guess I had a pretty good idea as to what I wanted to do. Fortunately, I was able to do that. You know, it doesn't happen all the time that way.

Johnny Pesky was instrumental in the Red Sox making a deal for me. I was going to fill-in where they needed help, at third base or shortstop. I think the first time I got to play was when George Scott broke his hand. I got to play about a month or so and played well.

I heard all these wonderful things from my teammate Mike Hegan about the Boston area, my wife was so hopped-up on New England before we got here. Right now, I don't think you could dynamite her out of New England. It's a beautiful place. You can drive a couple of hours and enjoy the beauty of the rocky coast in Maine or drive someplace and think you've traveled back 100 years in time.

30

Fred
Lynn

With the Boston Red Sox, Fred Lynn averaged 20 home runs, 85 RBIs and a .308 average in six often-sensational seasons. In 1975, a summer in which the center fielder earned 13 significant honors, Lynn became the first player to capture the Most Valuable Player Award and Rookie of the Year Award in the same season.

Born February 3, 1952, in Chicago, Lynn grew up in California and played on three NCAA championship teams at the University of Southern California where he was twice named to the College Baseball All-American Team by The Sporting News. On June 5, 1973, he was drafted by the Red Sox and later signed with Boston.

After marginal numbers in 139 minor league games, Lynn joined the parent Red Sox for 15 games in 1974, in which his .419 batting average foreshadowed what Red Sox fans would see the following year. That season, Lynn terrorized opposing pitchers as Boston won 95 games en route to the American League East title. On June 18, 1975, Lynn hit three *home runs and tied an AL record for most total bases (16) in a 15-1 victory in Detroit. Overall, Lynn set an AL record for most doubles (47) by a rookie, led the league in slugging percentage (.566) and runs scored (103), batted .331 with 21 homers and 105 runs batted in. Along with Jim Rice (.309, 22 homers, 102 RBIs), a new and powerful chapter in club history began.*

In the post-season, Lynn batted .364 in a three-game sweep of Oakland for the AL championship. In the World Series against Cincinnati, Lynn batted .280 but displayed his brilliance as a fielder. In Game 6, his first-inning, three-run homer spotted Boston an early advantage on a night made famous in the 12th inning by Carlton Fisk's homer down the left field line.

Lynn came back to bat .314 as a sophomore but was then nagged by various injuries. In 1979, Lynn recovered with another strong campaign—winning the batting title (.333) as well as clubbing 39 homers and driving in 122 runs. After batting .301 in 1980, Lynn was traded to California on January 23, 1981, with pitcher Steve Renko for pitchers Frank Tanana and Jim Dorsey and outfielder Joe Rudi. The swap brought embarrassment to the Red Sox—not over what amounted to a one-sided deal—but events leading up to the trade. The Boston front office, fearing salary arbitration, overlooked the tendering process date of December 20 in the standard player's contract when mailing Lynn his 1981 contract (the Bosox also missed the deadline with Fisk and Rick Burleson). When Lynn opted to challenge ownership by filing a grievance, Boston worked a deal with California.

With the Angels, Lynn never scaled the .300 plateau but averaged 22 home runs over three years before signing as a free agent with Baltimore on December 11, 1984. With the Birds, Lynn continued to extend his string of 20-plus homers and remained in Baltimore until August 31, 1988, when he was traded to Detroit for three minor leaguers. Lynn hit .241 in 117 games with the Tigers, declared himself a free agent at the end of the season and signed with San Diego for 1990.

Over 16 seasons, Lynn has batted .284 with 300 home runs. He has made only 53 errors in 1,879 games for a fielding percentage of .988. A nine-time All Star, Lynn was voted in by the fans as a write-in winner in 1975. In 1983, Lynn became the first player to hit a grand slam in the mid-season classic.

◆   ◆   ◆

My first year with the Red Sox was pretty much something from a storybook. I was just another rookie until the middle of June in '75. The local people, the writers and fans around Boston, knew who I was but not the national media—until I hit the three home runs in Detroit.

That can't happen now. If a guy gets off to a hot start, he's already in contention for the MVP Award. A while back, I had a reporter ask me about the young centerfielder now with the Red Sox. Ellis Burks was just breaking in. He had a good series against Baltimore and I was asked the question, "Do you think Burks could be Rookie of the Year?" Gee, Christmas! A guy has a couple of good games and already, they're touting him for Rookie of the Year! Not that something like that couldn't be, but that's what has happened to baseball.

I'm glad I came up when I did. I was ready to play right away, but to get to the major leagues, a young player must be mature enough to handle the lifestyle. There's more traveling, longer bus trips, staying in hotels, stuff like that. The ball playing is the easiest part. When you're in the minor leagues, it's tough. You don't have much money and you spend long periods of time on the road. At Southern Cal, we flew everywhere—first-class all the way.

My first year in pro ball, I played in Bristol. What I recall most was doing a lot of fishing when I wasn't playing ball. Jimmy Burton, Andy Merchant and I rented a cottage on Cedar Lake. We did catch some bass there.

I batted only .259 that season but I really liked the ballpark. Muzzy Field was a pretty place. It reminded me of playing in the woods because there were big, tall pines all around the outfield fence. It was built for left-handed hitters, yet I do recall Jim Rice smoking a few over the trees in leftfield.

One of the toughest things for me was getting used to the weather. Essentially, I'm a southern California kid. The temperature is ideal for baseball. No humidity at all. By the latter part of August, the weather got to me. I felt tired all the time. My performance in the field started to suffer. But, when I was sent up to Triple A to help Pawtucket in the playoffs, I got rejuvenated again.

When I first came to the big leagues, I felt 10 years would be a good timetable. At the time, the average stay for a player in the majors was about four years. I don't really know what it is now but it probably hasn't changed that much. You tend to see the same players every year but not everyone stays around. There is turnover in baseball but you don't realize it. There are so many guys no one ever sees. They're here for a month, a year or so, and then they're gone. There are hundreds of players like that.

I think it would be much harder now for a young guy coming into the big leagues. There is much, much more media attention. The game is blown up more because of TV coverage, statistics, things like that. Today, you can see what you're doing every day. I recall the only time you could see how every player was doing was in the Sunday newspaper. Now, every stat you can think of is published. Even at the ballpark! In Cleveland, you can make an out and, on your way back to the dugout, you can see your new average up on the scoreboard before you sit down. I don't like it.

Stats have never been a special goal of mine but considering how I hit in Fenway, I would have likely piled up higher numbers if I had stayed in Boston. One of the first times I took batting practice there, I was fooling around and I slapped an outside pitch to the opposite field. I heard this big "CLANK" when the ball hit the Wall. I did it again. Another "CLANK."

I certainly miss Fenway. I had to get used to hitting without the Wall. Every player has a slump and if I fell into one on the road, I'd go out early to the ballpark for some extra batting practice. I'd clang a dozen or so balls off the Wall and I'd be fine.

I would have liked to have spent my whole career in Boston. That would have been ideal. But, unfortunately, baseball is a business and I had to go away to get the best deal I could.

Fenway helped me as a hitter, but injuries have had a lot to do with my troubles the last few years. It's a cumulative effect of years of running into walls and diving on the ground from playing both football and baseball.

The fans in Boston always treated me well. The people are interested in baseball. I can say the same about the fans in Baltimore. They, too, can't wait for Opening Day. That's all they talk about all winter, "How are the Sox or O's going to do?" In California, it's "Can the Lakers win again?" "Can this new guy quarterback the Rams to the Super Bowl?" or "Let's go see the Beach Boys at the Forum."

31

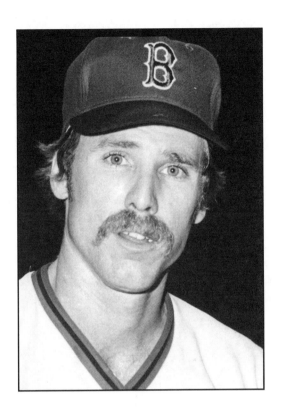

Steve Dillard

*T*he ability to play three infield positions enabled Steve Dillard to be a contributing player for six summers in the big leagues— including a two-year hitch with the Boston Red Sox.

Born in Memphis on December 8, 1951, Dillard grew up in Mississippi and was a standout at Saltillo High where he earned 16 letters. Highly recruited, Dillard earned a baseball scholarship to the University of Mississippi, a stepping stone to becoming Boston's second selection in the 1972 amateur draft.

Beset by arm injuries, Dillard was shifted from shortstop to second base in the minor leagues and made a cameo in Boston for the final month of 1975. Over the next two seasons, as the team's infield utilityman, Dillard played in 123 games, batting .260 with 21 doubles and two home runs. But when Boston acquired additional infield help, Dillard requested a trade and was shipped to Detroit on January 30, 1978, for pitchers Mike Burns and Frank Harris.

"I figured I might find some regular work," says Dillard who spent

1978 in Detroit. "As it turned out, I watched two good ones, Alan Trammell and Lou Whitaker."

The next stop was Chicago and at Wrigley Field, Dillard wound up having his best season. The Cubs purchased his contract from the Tigers on March 20, 1979, and Dillard responded with a .283 average and five home runs. He also won the National League's Player of the Week honors for August 7-12 with 12 hits in 20 at bats, including 11 runs batted in, nine runs scored and three homers.

Dillard remained with the Cubs through 1981 and finished up with the crosstown White Sox in 1982, winding up a career which consisted of 438 games and a lifetime .243 batting average. Following the season, Dillard went into managing and instructing in the minors, most recently with the Houston Astros organization.

◆　　　◆　　　◆

By my senior year in high school, a lot of scouts were following my progress, especially Ellis Clary who now works for Minnesota. Ellis is one of the game's real characters. He came to our area and must have stayed a week. I remember riding with him to a couple of games, just chewing the fat.

I thought for sure I'd get drafted by the Twins. Turns out, I was picked by San Diego, but it wasn't until a year or two later that I found out why Minnesota overlooked me. I got a note from Ellis with a newspaper article enclosed. His letter went something like "In case you're wondering why I didn't draft you, I had a heart attack." Ellis died three times on the operating table but the doctors were able to save him. I've seen Ellis several times since and you'd never know he ever had any health problems.

As much as I wanted to play ball, the best offer the Padres could make was that maybe I could room with Mike Ivie in rookie ball. I thought my dad was going to strangle the scout when he offered $3,000. I had a scholarship waiting and, weighing the offers, it was not a hard decision to make.

At Ole Miss, Jake Gibbs, who caught for the Yankees, was my coach. I started as a freshman and led the team in hitting. During the summer, I played in a good semi-pro college league in Liberal, Kansas, which was called the Ban Johnson League or something along those lines. We played every day, about 60 games or so, and some of the guys, Steve Bowling and Duane Kuiper to name two, ended up in the big leagues.

It was at Liberal that I hurt my arm. When I returned to school, Gibbs moved me to second base. The more games I played, the better I felt. One thing I remember him saying all the time was "You have to be loosey-goosey to play." One time, we played at Memphis State and the field was terrible. I made five errors. There had to be about 20 scouts in the stands that day. Jake just said to me, "Steve, all you can do is hang in there." He was telling me to relax. That made an impression on me.

I had a good year in 1972 and made a number of All Star teams. I wound up going pretty high in the draft and elected to sign. The Red Sox picked me as their second overall choice and assigned me to Winston-Salem in the Carolina League. I played around 50 games my rookie year. I found pitching to be the biggest adjustment between college and pro ball. In 1973, I came around and batted .279 with a little power.

Looking back at playing in the minors and even managing now, the team is like a little community. You go into an area and most of your time is spent with that group. You don't really get involved in the city or town affairs that much because you're playing virtually every day. The thing I remember about coming to Bristol was that the city did not have a hotel, only a couple of small motels. We were going on a road trip right away and I had to leave my family there and hope that my wife could find a place for us to live. The night we arrived, we were so hungry from driving, we were trying to find something to eat. All we kept seeing were these signs for "Grinders." I really had no idea what a grinder was. We finally stopped at one because it looked like an eating place. What we called subs or hoagies down South were what people up here call grinders.

With the Red Sox, I got a chance to watch Fred Lynn and Jim Rice, two outstanding but different type of players. Fred was a great center fielder, a line drive hitter with some power. Lynn batted .280 in Pawtucket with 22 home runs and then just went wild the next year in the big leagues, becoming the MVP and Top Rookie. Jim was a power hitter who hit for average and went to the big leagues fairly early in August in '74. Despite missing a month in Triple A, he still won the Triple Crown. He hit .330, Rob Andrews hit .306 and nobody else hit .300 in the whole league.

One time at Pawtucket, Rice was in a slump and he asked to use one of my bats. The one he wanted was a special order I had made for off-season training, hoping swinging it every day would improve my strength. It was 38 or 40 ounces and 36 inches long. I used it to loosen up before batting practice, too.

Well, Rice wound up using it in a game. He hit eight home runs with that bat in seven days.

I joined the Red Sox at the end of the '75 season when they were in a pennant race. Darrell Johnson was the manager and he was a smart baseball man. He taught me things that I try to pass on to the young players.

I remember Darrell saying, "If you come up with runners on second and third and nobody out, what are you going to be thinking at the plate?" All of us figured that the best thing to do was hit a fly ball to get the runner from third home, but we were off. "The best thing you can do is hit a ground ball to second base which scores the runner on third and moves the runner on second to third." That's the type of manager Darrell was. The little things were important.

Luis Tiant was the funniest guy I ever met and one pitcher who wasn't afraid to pitch inside. Tiant was always joking around the clubhouse. He could be taking a shower, be in the whirlpool or just relaxing and he'd always have a cigar in his mouth. One time in spring training, somebody just crushed one of his pitches to center field and he's yelling, "GO FOUL! GO FOUL!" Tiant would keep you laughing all the time. He went to the airport one day to pick up his parents when they were coming up from Cuba and he was carrying a big gun with him. He had a permit to carry one but as he went through one of those restricted areas at Logan, the beepers went off and security caught him. In Massachusetts, especially with the gun laws, it's a wonder they didn't put him in jail.

Everyone in Boston was really looking forward to '76 because of that great World Series against Cincinnati. For me, just being on a pennant winner was a great introduction to the major leagues. The season opened and we started off bad, something like 6 and 15. We lost 10 in a row on a road trip. We had rainouts, were snowed in at O'Hare and also got swept in Kansas City. We were so far behind, we couldn't catch up. Things didn't go as expected and when July came around, the Red Sox hired Don Zimmer. "Zim" was a colorful kind of guy. He could be outspoken when he had to be and was fun to play for.

That year, the Red Sox just never really got on track. I got sent down in August and played a month in Pawtucket. That's when Boston decided to make me a second baseman. There was no way I was going to beat out Rick Burleson. He was in the game all the time. What a fiery competitor! Rick was a guy who could play 160 games a year. I was a fill-in, someone who could play maybe 30 or 40 games.

I had two players ahead of me with the Red Sox, Jerry Remy and Denny Doyle. Doyle taught me a lot about playing the position, like the backhand flip and always being ready. You have to think about situations out there. Denny was real good and Remy was going to replace him. It didn't look good for me to make the team or to play much if I did stay with the varsity. The following winter, they worked a deal out with Detroit.

The Tigers had Tito Fuentes, who hit .300, but was released because they had a couple of kids coming out of Double A playing like houses afire, Alan Trammell and Lou Whitaker. Detroit didn't really have a second baseman so it looked like I was going to play and, for a while, Ralph Houk platooned us. Mark Wagner and I would play against righties and Trammell and Whitaker would play against lefties.

We had some good players there like Rusty Staub, Jason Thompson and Steve Kemp and a pitching staff with Jack Morris, Dave Rozema and Mark Fidrych. The "Bird" threw a couple of good games early in the season but his arm went out on him again. Bird was tried and true. He had so much energy, he wasn't putting on the dog at all. It was a shame that he had an arm problem. He would have been a very good pitcher and would have been good for baseball because he drew the fans. Everybody loved him.

Nowadays, you see more Dominican players who are good players. I recall reading a story recently about a scout driving through the country on a weekend and seeing eight baseball games going on. Kids in the States, it seems, are interested in television, computers and stuff like that. I'm not saying it's bad, but, it's tough to develop baseball players when they're not playing outside.

When I grew up, there wasn't anything else to do. You'd play cowboys and Indians or ride a horse on the farm. I grew up loving baseball and wanting to play. My theory on why the black athletes have had such an influence on baseball is because they were in the same boat I was in. There wasn't much to do growing up and if you play baseball, it gives you a chance to make something of yourself. They play and play and develop where maybe most white players are concerned about the game but don't feel the need to practice to improve. My younger brother loved to play in the games but he didn't want to go out and practice. He liked people to see him in his uniform, you know, and he wasn't alone. If you want to make it, you have to dedicate yourself. You have to play every day, work hard and really want it.

My dad never pushed me or my younger brothers into sports. We were all athletes but it bothers me to see some parents push their kids, the attitude being, "You gotta play Little League. You gotta win." I don't believe that. If a kid shows a desire in something, give him a chance to do it. If my kids want to play the piano, I'd give them that right. That's the way my dad was. He saw that I loved the game and he gave me everything he could, probably some things he couldn't really afford. He'd come home from work and the last thing he wanted to do was go out and play ball with his kids. He was on his feet all day long but he'd come home and hit grounders to me for an hour. I know that he probably would rather be doing something else but he gave me the time.

I spent some time in Chicago and Dave Kingman was truly unbelievable. In 1979, he hit 48 home runs and really carried us. We were about six games out in late August and then had a disastrous road trip to California and lost, I want to say, 11 of out 13 games. We just fell out of it. Everyone on the club cooled off hitting.

I saw Kingman hit three homers in one game at Wrigley Field. Each one was a little farther than the one before. I believe the stories I've heard about the time he hit one, where the ball landed on the front porch two or three houses down the street. He hit a home run one day to center field one-handed. He was out in front of the ball and just kind of flicked his wrist and the ball went 400 feet.

My best year was 1979 when I hit two home runs in one game and five over three weeks. There was a stretch of games, maybe for two or three weeks in August, that it seemed I did everything right. I waited for a good pitch and hit the ball hard. I don't really know how they arrive at who wins that Player of the Week Award but I earned it one week.

We had some talented players in Chicago. Everybody thought pitching was our weak spot but we had some people who were better than just average pitchers. We had Mike Krukow, Dennis Lamp, Rick Reuschel, Bill Caudill, Bruce Sutter, Lee Smith, Willie Hernandez and Donnie Moore. We had each one of them but the only thing I remember is they seemed to pitch better when they joined other teams. You'd be sitting in the dugout and somebody would be warming up in the bullpen. You'd see a ball come bouncing by and say, "Well, it must be Moore or Hernandez." Sure enough, it would be one of them. They'd go into a game and really get lit up. Willie came up with a screwball and Moore finally got some control. They got a chance to prove themselves later on.

Reuschel was a competitor. When you took the field on a day he pitched, you expected to win. Reuschel's theory on pitching was simple. If he threw a shutout, he'd win. If he gave up one run, he'd have a chance to win. If he gave up two runs, he'd probably lose.

Being an infielder, I loved to watch Ozzie Smith take ground balls in practice. He was just so smooth. Everything he did looked so effortless. He used a big old glove and just amazed me. He's one guy you'd just stop and watch take infield because he made unbelievable plays. He'd dive at a ball that would bounce up, recover and still throw the runner out.

The Cubs eventually cleaned house when Dallas Green came over and I was "designated for assignment" which means I was going to be released in 10 days. I ended up with the White Sox and was hoping to be their utilityman. Teams in the National League tend to keep two spare infielders. Mick Kelleher and I were in that role with the Cubs. Tony LaRussa was going to keep just one and take an extra outfielder. The White Sox had Greg Pryor, Pete MacKinnon and myself. They traded Pryor, released MacKinnon and sent me to Triple A when they acquired Vance Law.

I went to Edmonton and played in the Pacific Coast League and hit the ball better than I ever hit in my life. I eventually got up to the Sox. LaRussa, in my opinion, is the best manager in the business. He was on top of everything before it happened. He knew what he was going to do and he'd take the time to explain things to his players, his strategy for certain situations. I'd put him right up there with Earl Weaver, Billy Martin or Dick Williams for running a team.

32

Jerry
Remy

*S*econd baseman Jerry Remy played 1,154 games over 11 seasons in the majors and may have played several more but for a series of knee injuries.

"The knee wore down. Three operations really didn't help at all," says Remy, who had a career .275 average, stole 208 bases and played for the Boston Red Sox from 1978 to 1984. "If I had been a pitcher and had my shoulder worked on that many times, I would have never been able to play. Looking back, I feel extremely fortunate to have had an opportunity to play in the big leagues."

Born November 8, 1952, in Fall River, Massachusetts, Remy was a 19th-round pick by the Washington Senators in 1970, but he declined an offer to sign. He waited for the secondary phase of the amateur draft, was picked by the California Angels in January 1971, and inked a contract. With the Angels, Remy developed into a capable threat—with the glove, bat and on base because of his speed.

Remy spent four years in the minors before joining the Angels in 1975 *as the team's regular second baseman. With California, Remy stole 110 bases and averaged .258 over three seasons before coming to the Red Sox in a deal for Don Aase and cash on December 8, 1977.*

In his first year with the Bosox, Remy stole 30 bases, linked a 19-game hit streak and batted .278. He also led American League second basemen with 114 double plays, was second in total chances and was selected to the league's All-Star team.

Remy's next two years with Boston were hampered by knee injuries which limited his contributions over the second half of each year. In 1979, Remy was batting over .300 and what loomed as his best season virtually ended on July 1 when he hurt his left knee in a slide at home plate against the New York Yankees. A year later, against the Cleveland Indians, Remy tore cartilage in the same knee and missed the final 82 games.

In 1981, a season marred by the player's strike, Remy batted .307. In a 20-inning game on September 20 against Seattle, Remy equaled an AL record by collecting six hits. Although a free agent, Remy and the Red Sox agreed to a new, long-term contract. Regaining past form, Remy batted .280 in 1982 and then .275 in 1983. The following year, Remy played just 30 games as his weak knee gave out. He was placed on the disabled list on May 19 and after missing 1985 because of chronic problems with his knee, the Red Sox released him following the season.

In 1986, Remy worked as a minor league coach with Boston's Double A club in the Eastern League. Today, he is a television analyst on Red Sox games for the New England Sports Network.

◆   ◆   ◆

The most fun I ever had in baseball was in 1978. I came to Boston from California and was happy to be going to a team that had the talent to win the pennant. It was exciting to be around a team with players like Carl Yastrzemski and Luis Tiant.

Yastrzemski **was** the Red Sox. As a kid, I remember seeing him play. It was a thrill for me to get a chance to play on the same team with him. He was a competitive sonuvagun, too. When it came to hitting, Yaz was always trying to improve. He worked at it every day. Yaz wasn't the "rah-rah" type of guy in the clubhouse but he'd take charge in the field. When I saw Yaz make a great play against the Wall, I wanted to do the same. That's what I remember most about him. I know players move on and all but when you think of the Red Sox, you think about Ted Williams and Carl Yastrzemski. A big chunk of the Red Sox organization left the day he retired.

El Tiante was a real competitor, the type of pitcher who, if you made an error behind him, he'd come right up to you afterwards and say, "Don't worry. You win games for me, too." And, did Luis win games for us! He knew how to pitch and was the type of character every team needs. He knew when to make everyone laugh but he also knew when to be serious.

My first year in Boston, we just mashed teams. Batting second, I couldn't run as much as I wanted to because we had Fred Lynn, Jim Rice and all the rest of the thunder coming up. It didn't make sense stealing bases with Lynn, Rice, Yaz, Fisk, Dwight Evans and Butch Hobson waiting to hit. If we had a little more pitching, we may have won 120 games. As it turned out, we won 99 games and fell one game short.

There's a lot of talk about how we collapsed that year but that wasn't the case at all. We didn't play well for a stretch of games, that's all. Some of our key people got hurt, too. The thing everyone seems to forget is that there was a damn good club behind us – the Yankees.

When you have players like Graig Nettles, Lou Piniella, Thurman Munson, Reggie Jackson, Mickey Rivers, Willie Randolph, Chris Chambliss, Rich Gossage and whoever else they had, that's a good team, period. The Yankees were a club of professionals who knew how to play and how to win. They were like the Oakland clubs in the early 1970s. They played sensational baseball over the second half. We also made up a deficit in September. The season for both of us boiled down to one more game and we fell short by one run.

I've replayed that playoff game many times in my mind. To this day, I still wonder how Lou Piniella ever came up with the ball in the ninth inning. When the ball left my bat, I knew it was going to drop in for a hit. In all probability, the ball should have gone by him. At that time of the day in Fenway, the sun is tough on a right fielder. I'd like to say Piniella lost the ball in the sun but he made a heck of a recovery. If the ball got by Lou, Rick Burleson would have scored easily which would have tied the game. And with the way I could run, I'm on third with one out and we have Rice and Yaz due to hit. A fly ball and we win the game. As it turned out, we ended up with runners on first and second and Gossage, the best reliever in baseball, got us.

I don't think it would be fair to say the Red Sox never recovered from that loss but I'll say this – for a couple of years, that awesome feeling where you'd walk into any ballpark and knew you were going to beat somebody's brains out was gone. We were not competitive because free agency came along and the Red Sox lost a number of key players. When my turn came up, I wasn't sure the Red Sox were going to keep me. Why they chose to sign me and let the others go, I don't really know. Maybe I was in the right place at the right time. Maybe the pressure was such that they had to sign players.

Ralph Houk was the right guy for what was happening to the Red Sox. He was a master of handling the media. Houk did a good job of putting a positive feeling back in Boston during some negative times. In 1981, he got more out of a club than anyone thought. He developed some young kids, too.

I played 11 years in the big leagues and would have played longer if my knees held up. When I was healthy, I was able to play 150 games a year. Even after the injury, I was able to come back and play two full seasons. The first time I got hurt, even after months of therapy, my knee still bothered me. I went to spring training, played on it and my knee finally blew out on me in 1980. I felt fine after the operation but after playing on it again, everything just started to break down. Each winter I was going in for arthroscopic surgery. It finally got to a point where it didn't do any good.

I didn't have a great career but it was a good career. I have good memories of playing and I'm happy for getting the chance to play. I wanted to play baseball more than anything else. In high school, I concentrated on baseball because it was one sport where I felt I had a chance to play at a higher level.

I was just 18 years old when I went to spring training in 1971. Kenneth Myers, an old timer from the Dodgers organization, was a real red-ass of a coach. He always had a cigar hanging out of his mouth and was always on my case. I often wondered why he ever put a uniform on. He was all over me and I couldn't understand it. That man worked with me every day and really taught me the game of baseball. Later on, I realized that the Angels were going to release me but Myers wouldn't let them. All he said was "this little guy can run. I'll teach him how to play."

That was my start. With El Paso in the Texas League, long before the season ended, Dave Garcia made me believe I was going to be a major leaguer. At the time, Denny Doyle was playing second base for the Angels and he had been a regular for awhile.

"Who runs better," Garcia asked me one day, "you or Denny?"

"I do."

"Who throws better?"

"I do."

"Who hits better?"

"I do."

"Well, then, you're going to the big leagues."

What Myers and Garcia taught me was all worth it because by the time I went to spring training with the parent club, I was ready to play. Dick Williams was managing the Angels then and Williams was the best and the hardest manager I ever played for. It was basic, fundamental baseball–his way. If you didn't do the little things, you didn't play.

He was the moodiest man I have ever met but Williams knew baseball. After playing one year for him, I knew I'd never play for a guy as tough as him as long as I stayed in baseball.

We had a lot of talent in California but could never score enough runs to help the pitchers. And we had two of the best, Nolan Ryan and Frank Tanana. Ryan was just a blow-it-by-you pitcher but Tanana would have really been something if he didn't have arm problems. He'd be the pitcher I'd pick to win one game—before he hurt his arm. Frank was only a young kid but what control! He threw hard but also had a good curveball. He could do what most pitchers will never do. It took Frank a while to learn another way but he was able to do it because he always had an idea of how to pitch. It was common any time he pitched, the other team had two or three guys who would decline to play.

33

Ralph
Houk

When Ralph Houk returned from World War II combat his
teammates called him the "Major," the rank he attained.
With the 9th Armored Division, Houk fought at Bastogne
during the Battle of the Bulge and was awarded the Silver
Star, Purple Heart and Bronze Star.

Throughout his baseball career, the Major won his share of battles,
first as a catcher and then as a dugout boss with the New York Yankees,
the Detroit Tigers and the Boston Red Sox. Houk, who led the Yankees
to three American League pennants and two World Series championships
in his first three years as a manager, came out of retirement in 1981 to
skipper the Red Sox. Houk stayed through the 1984 season, a four-year
period best categorized as transitory. Recently, Houk served as a consul-
tant of baseball operations for the Minnesota Twins before retiring after
the 1989 season.

Born in Lawrence, Kansas, Houk turned down a college football
scholarship to play baseball. Although mostly a caddy for Yogi Berra,

Houk hit .272 in 91 games over seven seasons. He went on to manage 3,156 games over a 20-year hitch—the 10th highest total in the history of baseball.

◆   ◆   ◆

My first year managing the Yankees has to be my fondest memory in baseball—winning the pennant and the World Series. I can't talk about my playing ability because most of that was breaking in Yogi's gloves. It would be kind of foolish.

I've been fortunate in my career to manage in three towns that follow and know their baseball. New York, Detroit and Boston were a lot of fun. In Detroit and Boston, they had to change the ballclub and go with younger guys. We were doing real well toward the end and shortly after that, Boston made it to the World Series. The same is true in Detroit. Everywhere I've left, the teams have had success. Maybe if I stayed longer, I might have been fired. You never know.

I left managing with a good taste from wherever I was. I was always in a place where everything seemed to be run by baseball people and we all worked together. When I was in New York, Del Webb and Dan Topping were the owners. They were great to work for. Lee MacPhail came in and he's the guy I give a lot of credit for what I was lucky enough to do in baseball. Lee was a big booster of mine. In Detroit, John Fetzer was the owner and Jim Campbell was the general manager. We went through some tough times. In Boston, Haywood Sullivan and Mrs. Yawkey were simply great. We kept improving each year and that's what they wanted to see. They knew we were going to lose games but they also knew we had to make changes.

I also worked one year for George Steinbrenner and in all honestly, he was good to me. When I left, George told me, "You're making a terrible mistake. I'm going out to get ballplayers, no matter what it costs." At the time, I thought he was kidding but George went out and did it. A lot of people don't realize what he has done for baseball when he signed the Hunters and Jacksons. This year, he went out and signed Jack Clark. Regardless of what people say, he's had a lot to do with the success of the Yankees and you have to give him a lot of credit.

Some people think baseball has changed today but I never found it that way. The players do make more money but when they walk into a big-league clubhouse, they want to win, look good for themselves and their families. They're great athletes, competitive, or they wouldn't be playing baseball at this level. As a manager, when you are not winning, the biggest thing you have to have is patience. You have to recognize that not every player is a star. If you have enough patience, I think that it's better for the player. It's a tough road in the minor leagues and when the player gets to the big leagues, it's a different world. He has to go through a totally different atmosphere on how to do things. Patience is a big key but respect goes both ways. A player has to respect the manager and the manager has to respect the player. Not everyone has the same ability and you can't treat all players alike. You have to talk to some of them in the office. Others, you have to kick a little or pat them on the back a little. As long as you can have fun playing baseball, it's a lot easier.

My years in the service, I think, did a lot for me. In that environment, you learn to understand people under stress. Without a doubt, it helped. I knew the problems that young men have away from home, and I guess it reached the point where you can take the bad with the good a little bit better because you had gone through the service under combat conditions.

I always had a lot of respect for the players. Maybe because I wasn't a very good ballplayer, I understood a lot of the players that weren't that great. I always felt I wanted to manage like I would want to be handled. Most players are under 30 years old and you have to respect the problems they go through. I never felt I had to give the press all the problems and my players knew that. I tried to be honest with them, respect their problems. I know it is a lot tougher to be a ballplayer.

Roger Maris went through a lot, more than people ever realize. Roger was a very modest person and a lot different than some of the things that were written. He was an outstanding player and did the things to win the ballgame besides hitting home runs. When it came towards the end of the 1961 season, it became obvious that he had a chance to break Babe's record. We were still in the pennant race and the press would come in the clubhouse after a game, and ask him about the home run chase. That kind of bothered Roger and he asked the reporters to talk to the players who were instrumental in winning that day.

I think probably the biggest lesson I learned from Casey Stengel was in handling the press. That's a big job for a manager, one of the toughest jobs he has. People laughed at the way Casey talked but he always knew what he was doing. He once told me, "Never admit to the press that you're wrong. You know more about the game than they do, so always have a reason for what you did, even if you don't have one. Not too many can second-guess you because they don't know enough. Just be sure you give them a reason why you did something."

One time, Johnny Klippstein, a right-handed pitcher, was going against us and Casey sent up the wrong guy to pinch-hit. Casey didn't realize it until Ellie Howard walked into the batter's box. Well, Howard hit one into the seats and we won the game. My locker was outside

Casey's office and I could hear the writers asking him, "How come you sent up a right-handed batter to bat?" And Casey said, "He wears that fellow out." Well, one writer didn't recall Ellie getting that many hits off Klippstein. Casey replied, "He didn't get many hits but you should have seen the shots he hit off of him."

I don't know if Casey could get away with it today because they keep so many records with the computers but I used to use a little bit myself when the writers asked me why I did this or why I didn't do that. I'd say, "You probably don't recall this but he hit some shots off of him."

That reminds me about a game my first season against the Red Sox. Frank Shea was a rookie, too, and he had a big year with the 1947 Yankees. Shea threw right-handed and he had little hands for a pitcher. The way he threw the fastball, it always kind of sailed in on a left-handed hitter. It was nothing but a fastball. It wasn't that fast but it came in on you and Ted Williams had trouble with it.

We're playing at Fenway and Shea is pitching a real good ballgame. We're one run ahead in the last of the ninth with two outs and the bases empty. Williams is the hitter and Rudy York, a big home-run hitter, was on deck. We get two strikes and a ball on Ted with that inside fastball, but I also see Ted moving back in the box, getting away from the plate. He's going to get that inside pitch. To this day, I don't know why but I decided that if Ted was looking for the fastball that much, I was going to call for a changeup. I put the sign down and Shea just grinned. You could see he just loved the idea about fooling Ted. Well, old Frank threw it and Ted hit a shot back through the box about four feet off the ground. If it had hit Shea, it would have killed him. The ball went out to the center field corner and Williams winds up with a double. York then hits one into the screen for a two-run homer and we get beat.

In the clubhouse, Bucky Harris comes over and says, very slowly, "What was that pitch you threw Williams?" I said, "It was a change of pace."

Bucky said, "He sure changed the pace of it, didn't he?" Williams was the most amazing hitter I ever saw. He could hardly wait to get up to the plate. We didn't use batting gloves back then, just resin on the hands. In the on-deck circle, you could hear Williams twisting his hands on the bat, getting ready to hit. The sticky resin would creak, and I'd hear crick, crick and I'd think, "Oh, God, here he comes."

Williams was the best at waiting and hitting the ball almost out of your glove. He could wait that long and still have the strength to snap his wrists and really hit the ball. He was just unbelievable.

What I miss the most about baseball is going to the ballparks, especially the old ones. I still visualize the old Yankee Stadium, with its long fence, the monuments in center field, the big Ballantine scoreboard, and the facade around the upper deck. Fenway Park has that green wall in left which just stares back at you and the fans there are right on top of you. There's just a different atmosphere in the old ballparks. In some of the new ones, when you go into a dome stadium, you feel like you're onstage. The old parks have a certain amount of charm about them. They also smell like a ballpark.

34

Wade
Boggs

Wade Boggs has set himself apart from his contemporaries by a consistent ability to hit a baseball. Judging by the continued decline in batting averages, the "Hitman" of the Boston Red Sox is in a class by himself.

In 1989, Boggs became the first player since 1900 to link seven consecutive 200-hit seasons. The avalanche of hits enabled Boggs, a lifetime .352 hitter, to manufacture the third highest career batting average in baseball history—behind Ty Cobb and Rogers Hornsby, tied with Shoeless Joe Jackson—and a number of major league and Boston team records.

Born June 15, 1958, in Omaha, Nebraska, Boggs grew up in Tampa and was considered, in 1976, among the best schoolboys in Florida. A subsequent low-round draftee by the Bosox that year, Boggs signed a contract and his first season was the only summer of his pro career he failed to bat .300. After five more years of seasoning at various levels, Boggs was ready for the big leagues.

With the Red Sox, Boggs became a regular on June 25, 1982, when *third baseman Carney Lansford suffered an injury. It was then that Boggs, an ardent student of Walt Hriniak's hitting discipline, began to revise history. That season, he batted .349 which is the highest average ever compiled by a rookie. The following year, Boggs hit .361 and became the ninth Red Sox in history to win an American League batting crown.*

In 1984, Boggs could not overcome a poor start but he finished sharply and wound up third in the batting race (.325). The tempo was set for 1985, a campaign where Boggs reached base safely in 135 games to match Chuck Klein's major league mark and became the 12th player in history to collect at least 240 hits in a season (including an AL record 187 singles) en route to his second batting crown (.368). The following year, Boggs again won the batting title (.357) to help Boston capture the AL East Division flag. In post-season play, Boggs had a big two-run single to help Boston defeat California 8-1 and gain a trip to the World Series. Against the New York Mets, Boggs batted .290 (9-for-31) and would have scored the winning run in Game 6 if the Mets had not pushed across three runs in the bottom of the ninth to force a seventh game. In 1987 and 1988, Boggs again won batting titles (.357 and .366, respectively). But misfortune in two of the last three years has illustrated Boggs's skill, strength and incredible level of focus during difficult personal times. The sudden death of his mother in a car accident in mid-1986 forced the realization of mortality. When a reputed extra-marital affair became public in 1988 and threatened to break up his family and embarrass him and the Red Sox organization, Boggs refused to tumble. Boggs, who was hitting in the .340s when the scandal broke, wound up pushing his average up better than 26 points to win an unprecedented sixth batting title this century. He also led the league in runs scored (128) and bases on balls (125). By collecting 200 hits and walking over 100 times, Boggs shares the company of Hall of Famer Lou Gehrig as the only players in history to do it three consecutive seasons.

Entering 1990, Boggs, a perennial All-Star since 1985, vows to work at hushing critics, those who overlook his hitting and nag him about his lack of power. It might be hard for some to realize it but Boggs possesses a .480 career slugging percentage and a .435 lifetime on-base percentage (second to Ted Williams in Red Sox annals). Defensively, Boggs has a .961 career fielding average at third base. While his glovework may not draw comparisons to Hall of Famer Brooks Robinson (.971), few have.

◆   ◆   ◆

Early in my career, I let a fan at Yankee Stadium get on my nerves. He sat near third base, about five rows up, but I could never find him. This particular fan had missed our first series in New York. On our second trip in, he was a no-show for the first two games. I thought I was blessed.

During batting practice on Sunday, I'm fielding ground balls. I'm feeling pretty good when I hear the gaudy voice, you know, the type that carries to every section in the ballpark.

"HEY, BOGGS! THOUGHT YOU WERE SAFE. I'M BACK."

I throw a ball back and scan the area by our dugout. All I see is blank faces.

What this character would do, just before a ball would come towards me, is start yelling. He'd time it so that I couldn't look his way.

Joe Morgan hits another grounder at me. I position myself to field the ball. In the distance I hear my friend.

"BOGGS, YOU'RE A STIFF. A REAL BUM."

I throw the ball back to Morgan and touch my cap.

Again, I check the seats behind the dugout but it's a sea of white shirts. Everyone looks the same.

Morgan hits another ball, a bit slower this time.

"BOGGS, YOUR FIELDING AVERAGE IS AS HIGH AS YOUR BATTING AVERAGE."

As the ball is coming, I look up. The ball rolls past me but I finally matched the voice with a face.

I retrieved the baseball in short left and headed towards the dugout. Now, it was my turn to yell.

"HEY, YOU. COME HERE."

He looks at me, as much to say, "Who me?"

"YEAH, YOU. YOU'VE BEEN ON MY CASE EVERY YEAR I'VE PLAYED HERE. COME HERE."

Now, this guy has a couple of big friends with him. He leaves his pals and heads to the front row of box seats.

I told him to extend his right hand.

"Here's a baseball. Keep it."

Today, this guy is phenomenal. He yells for me every time we play in the Bronx.

To be successful, no matter what you do, you need to stay in a positive frame of mind. I suppose that's the main reason behind all my superstitions. I have rituals for positive reinforcements. Back in high school, I read in a magazine once that the *chai* sign was a Chinese symbol for good luck. It turns out that it also means life in Hebrew. I'll draw that in the dirt before each at bat. Even before I get to the plate, I've drawn 7:17 in the on-deck circle. That's the time I run sprints each day. The sequence of numbers also reminds me of going seven-for-seven. As strange as all this may seem, it's as important to me as eating chicken.

In the minors, especially Class A ball and when I was in Double A in Bristol, the salary was not the kind where I could afford filet mignon every night. Chicken was the most inexpensive way to go. When I started, I had it four times a week. For some reason, I'd perform well on those four days. I put two and two together. Maybe there's some luck there. I started to eat chicken seven days a week. In 1983, I won my first batting title. I've been eating chicken ever since.

As a hitter, the main thing is to keep getting better. I'm only 30 years old but people say I hit like guys who played in the 1920s and 1930s. Maybe I'm in the wrong era. Maybe I didn't come along early enough.

Truthfully, I thought 1983 was the best season I could possibly have. I was asked "If you hit .361, can you hit .400?" I don't know. The year George Brett hit .390, he played only 117 games. From May 15 to the end of the season, I hit .406 over 119 games. Maybe if I had a little better start, I could have made a run at it. The stretch really put a positive feeling in my mind about hitting .400.

I always felt that some day I would be fortunate to get an opportunity to play in the big leagues. People have wondered why I wasn't up there sooner considering all the good years I had in the minor leagues. My father always brings up a good point—maybe I wasn't ready. If I had arrived sooner, maybe I might not have had the success I have had. It's strange the way fate works. I could still be sitting on a bench somewhere if Carney Lansford had not run into Lance Parrish and broken an ankle.

I became property of the Red Sox in 1976. Boston picked me on the seventh round. I played shortstop in high school but all the scouts projected me as a third baseman. There was a stretch of time when a lot of people felt I couldn't play third base but I've worked hard at it. The only way to get better is to practice. The main thing I had to do, especially when I first came up to the big leagues, was learn the hitters and where to play them. I'd miss a ball by one or two feet and the refrain I heard was "he doesn't have any range." I don't hear that anymore.

I broke into pro ball out of high school. I was 17 years old when Boston sent me to Elmira of the New York-Penn League. I was scared to death. It was only a 70-game season but I was competing against players with college experience and also playing every day. That was the biggest adjustment.

In high school, we played on Tuesday and Friday. Looking back, I had a frustrating season my senior year at H.B. Plant High. As a junior, I made the All-State team as a shortstop and led the conference in homers and RBIs. My father hinted my last season was going to be testy. He said opposing teams would pitch around me and he was right. I was walked with the bases loaded because coaches would rather concede one run than four.

For the first 10 games of the season, I had a lot of walks but just four hits in 27 at bats. I was having a rough time but my dad found the solution. He went to the library on Friday and checked out Ted Williams's book, *The Science of Hitting.*

"By Monday morning, I want you to know this book forwards and backwards," he said.

The main thing I learned from the book was patience and discipline. Get a good pitch to hit. Don't swing at a pitcher's pitch. That's what I tried to do. I wound up going 28-for-37 for the remainder of the season.

My dad remains my driving force. One year, he called at 1 o'clock in the morning and started yelling at me over the telephone. He had just watched a game from the West Coast where he picked up the Red Sox broadcast off his satellite dish in the backyard.

"Dad, what's the matter," I said.

"What are you doing?" he said. "Why are you opening up your stance?"

"What are you talking about?"

"I watched the game against the Angels the other night and you were opening your stance."

"Dad, I haven't changed my stance."

"Look, son. I know your stance better than you do. Do I have to send a tape of it to you?"

"Dad, what channel were you watching?"

"Channel 5. KTLA."

"That explains it."

"Explains what?"

"Dad, the camera angle in Anaheim is a few feet to the left side of dead center."

My father is really something. He has tapes of games and compares my swing each year. He's hard to satisfy at times. We'll get on the phone and he'll say, "Son, you went 3-for-4. Why did you swing at that pitch you lined to left?" He never talks about the hits. The conversation is short when I go 4-for-4.

Each year is different but 1985 was special for me. You try and put personal goals behind the team goal of winning but that year, we had a real disappointing season. What was left was individual honors and I was shooting for 240 hits. With 11 games to play, I needed something like 19 hits to get the highest total since 1930.

On the last day of the season, I needed three hits. Before the game, John McNamara, who was managing the Red Sox at the time, asked me, "How many at-bats do you want?"

"I'll go 3-for-3 and come out of the game," I said.

The first time up, I got a hit.

The second time up, I made an out.

When I was putting my bat in the rack, McNamara asked, "Do you still want to play?"

"Definitely," I said.

My next at-bat, I got another hit.

Around the sixth inning, McNamara says to me, "I didn't realize it, but right now, you're tied with Rod Carew. Do you want to hit again?"

"Just give me another at-bat."

I came up for the fourth time and I got a hit. I get down to first base and Eddie Jurak came in to run for me. I went 3-for-4 and the season was history.

Hitting is like feeding the computer. You form a memory bank and try to remember the negative things as much as the positive things. If a pitcher got me out two years ago, you remember the count and where he got you to hit the ball.

Recall Dave Righetti's no-hitter against the Red Sox on July 4, 1983? He struck me out to end the game but I also hit two line drives to center where, if Jerry Mumphrey had been playing center field instead of Dave Winfield, they might have been hits. Winfield shades me to right and Mumphrey shades me towards left-center. From my standpoint, though, if I did get a hit that day, I wouldn't have gotten out of New York alive.

35

Carl
Yastrzemski

*E*veryone knows you can't play forever, but few have come as close
as Hall of Famer Carl Yastrzemski.

Among baseball's litany of records, the name Yastrzemski
is frequently found among the game's all-time greats. Here's a
statistical glimpse of achievements compiled by Yaz during his tenure with
the Boston Red Sox from 1961 to 1983:

• Holds the record for most games played in American League annals
(3,308) and ranks second in major league history to Pete Rose (3,562);

• Holds the American League record for most at-bats (11,988) and
most plate appearances (13,990);

• Ranks as the first player in American League history with 400
homers and 3,000 hits;

• Holds the major league record for leading outfielders in assists
(seven different times);

• Ranks as the only player in baseball history to get 100 or more hits
in his first 20 seasons;

• *Became the first Little League baseball product to reach the Hall of Fame;*

• *Ranks third overall in reaching base (via hits and walks) to Pete Rose and Ty Cobb.*

In addition, Yaz is fourth overall in walks (1,845), fifth in total bases (5,539), sixth in doubles (646), seventh in hits (1,816) and extra-base hits (1,157) and ninth in runs batted in (1,844).

Born August 22, 1939, on Long Island in the then farming village of Southampton, Yastrzemski was signed by Red Sox scout F.J. "Bots" Nekola after one year of college at Notre Dame. After two solid minor league campaigns, Yaz joined the parent club as Ted Williams's successor in left field. As a rookie in 1961, Yaz struggled with the thought of replacing a legend. Overcoming a difficult start, Yaz finished strong, batting .266 in 148 games.

Over the following seasons, Yaz would win three batting titles (1963, 1967 and 1968) and finish with a .285 lifetime batting average with 452 home runs. His best year was 1967 when he became the 11th player in history to win the Triple Crown, leading the Red Sox to their first pennant in 21 years by batting .326 with 44 home runs and 121 RBIs.

In trying to capsulize his own career, Yaz rates helping the Bosox to the American League championships in 1967 and 1975, his retirement day in Boston in 1983 and enshrinement at Cooperstown in 1989 as his greatest thrills. He says his biggest disappointments were the seven-game defeats to St. Louis and Cincinnati in the World Series along with the 1978 playoff setback to the New York Yankees.

"I just hope I represented Boston and New England with class and dignity," says Yaz. "I might not have had the greatest ability but I tried to get most out of what I had."

◆　　　◆　　　◆

Those first few years with the Red Sox were depressing. We'd draw 700,000 fans a year, maybe 8,000 for a weekend game. But in '67, everything turned around.

The "Impossible Dream" was a season that not only turned on the fans but I think turned the Red Sox organization around. The Red Sox became winners instead of losers. The players expected to go out and win. The attitude in the clubhouse was just unbelievable.

That year was a transition one for me as a hitter. Up to that time, I was a gap hitter, to left-center and right-center. I was hitting for average but Bobby Doerr suggested that I raise my hands real high, about to my ear, to get more lift on the ball. In batting practice, I was hitting balls into the bleachers. There's a difference between BP and game time but I decided to try it. In a doubleheader against the Tigers, I hit two home runs. I stayed with that stance.

Hitting was never easy for me. It took total concentration, every game and each time at bat. It started in BP where you gear up for the game. You keep reminding yourself to stay focused on the pitcher and watch the ball. Go into the ball soft but don't overswing. Looking back, I did that over and over and that's what helped me to what I feel was my finest hour. . . the last six weeks of the '67 season.

Being compared to Ted Williams almost broke me. I sat in the clubhouse doubting my ability and thinking that maybe I couldn't play in this league. I was only 20 years old and they were calling me the next "Teddy Ballgame." A double wasn't good enough; I had to hit home runs. It got to a point where I was trying to be Ted Williams, not Carl Yastrzemski. The Williams thing was an albatross but it toughened me.

About two months into the season, I was hitting .220 and was about ready to cry when Mike Higgins said to me, "Kid, don't let it get you down. Just relax. You're my left-fielder every day, no matter what."

Mr. Yawkey knew I was struggling, too. I asked him one day if he could help. "I've got to talk to Ted," I said. "Can you get a hold of him?" Mr. Yawkey said that Williams was fishing somewhere in New Brunswick but he would do his best to contact him.

A day later, Ted showed up. I took a lengthy batting practice. Ted never said anything about changing this or that in my swing but he just built me up mentally. Ted stayed around two days and had me believing I could hit any pitcher. He gave me confidence that I could play in the big leagues. From that point on, no matter the situation or any at-bat, no pressure ever bothered me again.

I've often been asked about how ballplayers, as people, are able to stand up to pressure-packed situations and rigors of big league baseball? I've always answered the same way. Pressure? What pressure? Pressure is what faces millions and millions of fathers and mothers trying to earn a living every day to support a family and give it comfort, devotion and love. That's what pressure really is. That's what my parents gave me.

I know I couldn't have had any success in baseball or entertained thoughts about the Hall of Fame if it were not for the sacrifices made by my father who gave up his own career in baseball to work and raise his children. Growing up on a farm, because of the lifestyle that goes with it, lent itself to dedication and discipline. You had to work hard or you would not get the job done to have time for recreation. My father was an inspiration to me. He was my first manager when I played Little League ball. When I played semipro ball, he outhit me. I batted .420; he hit .440.

The biggest thing about what going to the Hall of Fame really says is that you were one of the best to play the game. Joining the greats like Babe Ruth, Lou Gehrig, Willie Mays, Hank Aaron, Ted Williams and Stan Musial is a great thrill. A lot of them were my heroes. My biggest is still Musial. I remember watching him play at Ebbets Field. He'd hit shots off the brick wall.

The day I was elected, one Boston columnist wrote it best. Tim Horgan interviewed one of my daughters and she said something simple. "Dad will always be remembered."

36

Roger Clemens

*I*t has not taken long for baseball fans to include "Rocket" Roger Clemens among the game's great hurlers. The tall right-hander's ability to throw 90-mph fastballs for strikes is a major reason the Boston Red Sox have become a franchise capable of winning a championship.

In 1987, Clemens became the fourth pitcher—and the first since 1976—to win consecutive Cy Young Awards. Though his string of awards ended in 1988, Clemens still ranked as the game's best pitcher according to baseball's statistical service. That season, his 291 strikeouts led the American League and broke Smoky Joe Wood's club record which had stood since 1912.

Born in Dayton, Ohio, August 4, 1962, Clemens grew up in Houston and developed into an All-American while at the University of Texas. In 1983, after leading the Longhorns to the NCAA championship, the Red Sox made Clemens the 19th overall selection in the amateur draft. In less than a year after turning pro, Clemens was in the big leagues.

◆ FENWAY VOICES

Despite a combined 16-9 record during Clemens's first two years, ailments to his right forearm and right shoulder limited his effectiveness. Following surgery, Clemens powered the Red Sox to the 1986 American League pennant by becoming the first moundsman in history to capture the Cy Young Award, league Most Valuable Player and All-Star Game MVP in one season. Clemens posted a 24-4 record with a 2.48 earned run average. Among the performances was a historic one against the Seattle Mariners at Fenway Park on April 29. That night, the "Rocket" established the major league record for strikeouts (20) in a nine-inning game.

It was, Clemens reflected later, the first time a team sold more tickets during a ballgame than at the start. There were less than 8,000 in Fenway when Clemens threw his first pitch. As each inning passed, the crowd, like strikeouts, kept growing in number. The gate that historic night was 13,414.

Though the Red Sox and Clemens were webbed in a series of contract squabbles in 1987, the sides finally agreed to a settlement upon the urging of Baseball Commissioner Peter Ueberroth. Despite a 20-9 season, Clemens could not rescue a ballclub which finished a quiet fifth, six games under breakeven.

In 1988, Clemens was among the contributors to Boston's second divisional crown in three seasons with an 18-12 mark and a 2.93 ERA. On September 10, he tossed a one-hitter against Cleveland, missing a perfect game in the eighth inning when Dave Chalk lined a single to right. In 1989, Clemens posted a 17-11 record and a 3.13 ERA. He struck out 230, second best to Nolan Ryan of Texas.

◆   ◆   ◆

When you're playing professional baseball, it is easy to lose track of time. You have a job to do and you just go out there and do it. You don't think you're involved in history but no matter what you do, it's recorded, every strikeout and every balk.

I have great respect for baseball history and what players before me accomplished. When I signed with the Red Sox, my mom set me straight, especially about Boston. She is a big fan of the Red Sox and told me about all the great pitchers the franchise has had over the years. That's why I'm glad I met Smoky Joe Wood.

I was only a rookie but I talked to Smoky Joe a short time before he passed away. He was at Fenway in a wheelchair for an Old Timers Game. It was really neat to hear him tell me about his days in baseball. Not a lot of the guys gave him the time of day, but I realized—not only for myself, but the tradition of when he played for the Red Sox and all the things he had done—I had to talk to him.

Smoky Joe set a bunch of records for this franchise and one of my highlights in 1988 was being able to break his strikeout record. It seems every time I break a team record, they show highlights of the two of us. It is really special to me. I'm not a big talker about a lot of things but the team strikeout record is a big thrill because it stood for a long, long time.

No matter what you do, the writers say what they want. It's easy, I guess, for them to get accustomed to what I've been able to do. Sometimes, in the heat of a pennant race, things will get overlooked. The only way you hear about something is when a reporter will say, "You're coming up on a record." It's a thrill when you can top someone else's achievement, especially when you break a mark set by one of the game's great pitchers.

Playing for the Red Sox involves a lot of tradition. To a degree, it reminds me of my college days. We had a good baseball tradition at the University of Texas. That's one thing I enjoy about Boston. The fans are so knowledgeable. They understand the game and that makes it fun. When people are aware of the intricacies of the game, the whole experience is that much more enjoyable.

I realize that I make a living entertaining people. A big part of what makes baseball so popular is the media. Baseball means so much to so many people, it's important to present yourself in the best manner. When I first came to the big leagues, I didn't realize that. I thought if I played the game and did my best every day, that was enough. I didn't have to worry about anybody but myself and the team.

I love to play baseball and I owe things back to the game. Every pitcher dreams about the Hall of Fame. If you are competing at this level, you have to be at your best or you won't stay around.

I'd like to be consistent, like Jack Morris, and keep putting up the numbers like he has over the 80s. Morris didn't have a typical year in 1988, but he's a pitcher who has been consistent throughout his career. Once you get to a certain level, you just try to maintain that. That's something I'm striving to do.

I know that I won't be able to throw the ball past people forever. The time will come for me, like it has for many others, when I'll have to make adjustments. When the time does come, I want to be in the best physical shape I can. I want to be able to still have endurance and the stamina I'm accustomed to having.

For me to be effective, I must do what's necessary, especially my running. I need strong legs. You can't be a strikeout pitcher without strong legs, but it's how you use them that makes the difference. I drive off my back leg but nobody, I think, will ever get the leg drive Tom Seaver did. He was one of a kind.

The one-on-one confrontation differs for each hitter, and I'm pretty intense on the day I pitch. I have to keep it that way to be the best I can be. I will get up for certain hitters, though. It's just that way. If it is someone like George Brett, Don Mattingly or Reggie Jackson in there against me, I'm a little more keyed up. Big names, you know, put a lot of great numbers up to get that big name.

I've played pro baseball a short time but winning at every level prepares you for the big leagues. Everyone has stepping stones in a career. Helping Texas to the NCAA championship in 1983 was just one of them. My first year with the Red Sox was just as important. After I signed and reported to Winter Haven of the Florida State League, I was pretty excited when I got the call to Double A. The main reason I didn't make the jump to Triple A was because the Pawtucket club was playing pretty poorly and the Red Sox wanted to keep me in a winning environment.

When I joined New Britain, the team was about six games out of playoff contention. Rac Slider put me right in there and I ended up doing some very positive things. I pitched pretty well and was real fortunate that I was able to accomplish what I did. As a team, we came from behind to make the Eastern League playoffs and wound up knocking off Reading and Lynn to win the championship. It was a great experience for me. I don't believe it's fair to say I was a leader on that team because they were on their way when I joined the ballclub. They just gave me the ball and I did the best that I could to win.

I'm proud of winning the Cy Young Award in consecutive years because no one has done it in the free agent era, so I feel as if I've done something significant. Sandy Koufax, Denny McLain and Jim Palmer were others who did it before me and that is pretty select company. Koufax is in the Hall of Fame, Palmer will be some day and McLain had two of the greatest years any pitcher has ever had.

The awards are nice and all but I want another opportunity to pitch in the World Series. To achieve every player's goal of being elected to the Hall of Fame and, personally, to be recognized as one of the best pitchers in the history of the game, that is essential.

About the Author

BETTY P. TRACY PHOTO

Jack Lautier, whose range around first base has greatly diminished with each passing summer, has covered the gamut as a sportswriter in Connecticut for a variety of newspapers and wire services.

Lautier, an award-winning journalist, has entertained *Bristol Press* readers daily since 1976. His first book, *15 Years of Whalers Hockey,* was published in 1987 and chronicled the history of the Hartford Whalers of the National Hockey League.

Besides books, Lautier is a frequent contributor to national publications such as *The Sporting News* and *Goal Magazine* and regional voices including *Connecticut's Finest* and *Hartford Monthly.* Jack and his wife, Janice, and their son, Patrick, reside in Southington, Connecticut.